KURDO BAKSI

STIEG LARSSON,
MY FRIEND

Translated from the Swedish by Laurie Thompson

MACLEHOSE PRESS
QUERCUS · LONDON

First published in Great Britain in 2010 by

MacLehose Press
an imprint of Quercus
21 Bloomsbury Square
London WC1A 2NS

First published in Sweden as *Min vän Stieg Larsson* by Norstedts, Stockholm, 2010
Copyright © by Kurdo Baksi, 2010

ISBN (HB) 978 0 85705 021 2
ISBN (TPB) 978 0 85705 071 7

10 9 8 7 6 5 4 3

Set in Cycles by Libanus Press Ltd, Marlborough
Printed and bound in Great Britain by Clays Ltd, St Ives plc

CONTENTS

1

The end and a beginning

Stieg Larsson's funeral took place on Friday, 10 December, 2004, in the Chapel of the Holy Cross at Forest Cemetery in southern Stockholm. The chapel was packed with relatives, friends and acquaintances. We filed past the coffin to pay our respects. Most of us whispered a final message as we walked slowly past the bier.

On the back of the order of service was a poem by Raymond Carver, "Late Fragment", from the collection he completed shortly before his death:

> And did you get what
> you wanted from this life, even so?
> I did.
> And what did you want?
> To call myself beloved, to feel myself
> beloved on the earth.

When Carver was asked how he wanted to be remembered, he replied, "I can think of nothing better than to have been called an author." Not many of the congregation in the chapel that afternoon would have realized that the same applied to Stieg. That he would be remembered as the author of one of the biggest, least expected publishing successes of modern times. For most of us he was a tireless hero in the fight against racism – there was no battle for democracy and equality that he was unwilling to take part in. He was aware that there was a high price attached to doing so, but it was a price he was prepared to pay. The constant threats, the lack of financial resources and the sleepless nights. It was a struggle that shaped his whole life.

But Stieg became an author – thanks to the capriciousness of life and death – only when he was no longer with us.

That afternoon we attended an uplifting memorial ceremony at the Workers' Educational Association in Stockholm, a venue at which Stieg had been keen to lecture ever since the publication of his first book, *Extremhögern* (The Extreme Right), in the spring of 1991. Tributes came thick and fast, delivered by, among others, his father, Erland Larsson, his brother, Joakim Larsson, his partner, Eva Gabrielsson, the publisher of *Expo* magazine, Robert Aschberg, the publisher-in-chief at Norstedts, Svante Weyler, the historian Heléne Lööw, Graeme Atkinson from the British magazine *Searchlight* and Göran Eriksson, the head of the Swedish W.E.A. I was master of ceremonies.

After the memorial ceremony we repaired to Södra Teatern, the theatre in the Söder district of southern Stockholm, a favourite haunt of Stieg's in his last years, for a funeral feast. It was icy cold on the terrace; the December chill froze us through and through. We shared our grief – family, friends, acquaintances and the entire staff of *Expo*. It was late at night before we broke up. We trudged home, each of us with our own memories of Stieg etched indelibly on our minds.

That was when the really difficult part began. Mourning in private.

"Farewell" is a hard word to define. Who is saying farewell to whom? The one who leaves or the one who stays behind? I keep coming back to that question over and over again. Of course I have lost a lot of friends and acquaintances over the years, but Stieg was my first really close friend to die. I set myself very high standards while grieving, but found myself groping around helplessly even so. I didn't know how to mourn with sufficient intensity.

After a while I realized that my memory was failing me. I forgot the names of people, lost my sense of direction, became anxious and depressed. But all the while the same message was pounding away at the back of my mind: I had to be strong. Stieg's partner, Eva, and the young members of the *Expo* staff needed me. I couldn't let them down now. I must not burst into tears in front of friends and acquaintances. I had learned a lesson from my time in the mountains of Kurdistan during the freedom struggle there: there is a time to weep, and a time to maintain a stiff upper lip and do whatever needs to be done.

I realized that I had to compromise. For a long time I avoided *Expo* and the places where Stieg and I used to meet: Il Caffè, Café Anna, Café Latte, the Indian restaurants on Kungsholmen and McDonald's in St Eriksgatan. Eventually I began to behave in exactly the opposite way. I wore black and made a point of going to the places I used to frequent with Stieg. It wasn't that I imagined we were sitting there together. It was rather a case of going there in order to come to terms with my own situation, irrespective of whether I actually wanted a meal.

Months passed. Eventually the day came when the first reviews of *Män som hatar kvinnor* (Men Who Hate Women, in English called *The Girl with the Dragon Tattoo*) were published. I eagerly devoured every word and was overwhelmed by a strange feeling:

I took everything that was said about the book personally. I began to regard myself as a sort of stand-in for Stieg. The reviews were almost exclusively positive, which pleased and distressed me at the same time. I was pleased by the thought that the books were going to be read by a lot of people, distressed because Stieg wouldn't be able to experience this for himself.

Eventually the first anniversary of that awful day came round. Rain pelted remorselessly against the windowpanes during the night of 8 November. My flat was only a stone's throw from Stieg's house. I was overcome once more by a tidal wave of sorrow and longed to be able to talk to him. I wished I could tell him that I was in love with a woman I knew he had met at one of the parties we had attended together. But there was only silence. I sat there, staring at the black and white tie Stieg had worn the last day of his life, the one Eva had given me as a keepsake. He should be close by, I thought, but he felt so dreadfully far away.

Maybe that was the moment when it finally came home to me that he had left us for good. I would never see him again. That night I made up my mind to travel to Skelleftehamn, the town in northern Sweden where he had been born, and to Umeå, where he had grown up. I bought plane tickets and prepared for the journey, but when the departure day dawned I realized that there was no chance of my travelling. Perhaps I'd be able to cope later on, but not yet. In fact I turned down several assignments in places close to his home territory: I still wasn't up to it.

Stieg's success as a writer did more than continue; if anything, the second volume in the Millennium trilogy, *Flickan som lekte med elden* (*The Girl Who Played with Fire*), was even more of a triumph. People in the trade began to talk about the most successful Swedish books of all time – and the third volume, *Luftslottet som sprängdes* (*The Girl Who Kicked the Hornets' Nest*), hadn't even been published yet. Stieg's name appeared in the newspapers almost every day; people on buses and in the underground had their heads buried in his books. He was still a constant presence in my life.

It struck me how little I actually knew about Stieg's existence before we met. He hardly ever mentioned the first twenty years of his life during all the time we were good friends. I began to wonder if something had happened in his youth that made it difficult for him to be in the spotlight. He always refused to think of himself as important in any respect. On the other hand, he thought a lot of other people were important.

Who was Stieg?

I wrote that question down on a piece of paper and stared at the words. It suddenly occurred to me that the reason he worked himself to death might be hidden away in his past. The fact is that even if we try to persuade ourselves otherwise, no human being is capable of working like Stieg did. Did he do it in an attempt to achieve ambitious goals he had set himself, or was it some kind of escapism? It may sound odd, but I really do believe that Stieg often thought he could change the world single-handedly if he only worked hard enough at it. I sometimes used to feel guilty because I myself was in favour of gradual change, while he could only feel at ease when he was working flat out. I have never met anybody with such a compulsive drive to work, such strength and energy.

*

Once I had asked myself that question – who was Stieg? – I noticed how the journalist in me was slowly but surely aroused once more. I started researching his early life and scanning the local newspapers *Västerbottens Folkblad* and *Västerbottens Kuriren*. Every day I learned something new about him – his homes in Hagmarksvägen and Ersmarksgatan in the Sandbacka district of Umeå, his years at the Hagaskolan primary school, then the Dragonskolan grammar school. I searched for his name in driving-school records, even though I knew he didn't have a licence. Perhaps it was a decision he had made early on without realizing the implications: the first piece of advice the police give to an individual living under threat is not to own a car, because the easiest way to track someone down in Sweden is through the driver and vehicle licensing authority.

When I discovered that Stieg had worked as a dishwasher at Sävargården in Umeå, I telephoned the well-known restaurant; none of the current staff had been working there at the same time. I was astonished to learn that he had completed his two years of national service with the I20 infantry regiment in Umeå. It is almost impossible to imagine Stieg as an infantryman. More credible was a spell as a manager at the pulp mill in Hörnefors.

Slowly but surely I worked my way back in time; it was like fitting together the pieces of a jigsaw puzzle. Almost before I knew where I was, I found myself in Östra Valliden and Varuträsk, just outside Skellefteå. There I got to know about a boy whose father had died and so had found himself in a foster home. This was Stieg's maternal grandfather. His first job was as a farmhand; then, like so many of his contemporaries in the 1920s, he worked as a navvy, building roads, or as a lumberjack. In his free time he hunted game in the forests or fished in the lakes around Bjursele.

His name was Severin Boström. It became obvious to me that in order to know Stieg Larsson, you needed to become acquainted with his maternal grandfather. People in Ursviken said of Severin that he was "a very passionate man". He had moved to Ursviken, between Skellefteå and Skelleftehamn, in order to run an engineering workshop. He repaired chainsaws, mopeds and bicycles. As soon as he could afford it he bought a car. During the Second World War, like so many people in those northern parts, he became a devout anti-Nazi. In his case, his convictions were so strong that they were a key influence on his notion of right and wrong.

One summer's day in 1953, at a dance in the People's Park in Skellefteå, Severin's daughter Vivianne met a man by the name of Erland Larsson, who was on a fortnight's leave from his military service. They fell in love, and a year later, on 15 August, 1954, the young pair had a son: Karl Stig-Erland Larsson.

It was far from easy for a young couple to make a living in those days. For a while Stieg's grandfather and father both worked at the Rönnskär sawmill, but before long Erland and Vivianne decided to seek their fortune in Stockholm, realizing that they would be forced to leave their one-year-old son with his maternal grandparents near Nordsjö.

It was 1962 before the family could be reunited. By then, Stieg had acquired a younger brother, Joakim, born in 1957. They all moved into a new home in Umeå, where Vivianne worked in a clothes shop and Erland was employed as an interior decorator for the clothes chain Berlins, which had shops in central Umeå, Skellefteå, Piteå and Örnsköldsvik.

While I was tracing Stieg's past, I frequently felt a kind of kinship with him. I was also forced to move house frequently because of my father's political activities. I like to think that children who grow up in such conditions develop a blend of rootlessness and restlessness. Combine those qualities with curiosity and you have a mixture that can be extremely important for a journalist later in life; but when you are a child, you often feel very much alone in the world.

As a teenager I ended up in Tensta, in Greater Stockholm, in a new country and without any friends. Stieg had also moved there only a few years previously – for him it was the same country, of course, but coming from Västerbotten in the remote north no doubt caused him his fair share of culture shock.

When we first met, as adults, Stieg and I had one thing very much in common: we had very few close friends.

With hindsight I have often thought that the restlessness we shared was an important reason why we got on so well together. When you have few friends around you, you often develop interests that fit well with your situation. In Stieg's case, films and the night sky were of great importance. Erland had a job for a while as the caretaker of a cinema, so Stieg and his younger brother were often able to sneak in and watch films. Stieg loved to immerse himself in this make-believe world, entranced by the captivating happenings on the silver screen. The same thing applied to his star-gazing, the heavens a grand mystery of which an individual could never experience more than a tiny fraction.

When Stieg celebrated his twelfth birthday he was given a

Facit typewriter and a telescope. These were by no means cheap presents, probably costing a lot more than his parents could afford. For Stieg, it was the fulfilment of a dream. One of his diaries contains several entries like this one: "1/2.1968, P.S. We spent a quarter of an hour searching for Uranus, without success."

It was around this time that Stieg became interested in politics, despite still being so young. His mother had become increasingly involved in trade union work and was soon a member of the local housing committee, active on the Disability Council and one of the founders of the first local authority equality committee. It was at this time that Stieg met Eva Gabrielsson, who was to become his partner. The occasion was a 1972 rally of the National Liberation Front protesting against the Vietnam War.

A friend of his told me that Stieg was also a keen photographer as a teenager – but the pictures were not the usual family snaps: he took photographs "in order to record injustice in the world".

Umeå soon became too small for Stieg. He had big ambitions. At the age of seventeen he hitched a lift on a long-distance lorry to Stockholm, and from there set off for Algeria. He had raised the necessary money by taking temporary jobs as a newspaper delivery boy and a dishwasher. But he didn't get very far: he was mugged, lost all his travel money and had to return to Umeå. Nevertheless, being the stubborn mule that he was, he worked hard to raise the funds for another attempt. This was the beginning of a series of long journeys. He finally reached Algeria and sold his leather jacket in order to be able to prolong his stay. After a two-year gap to do his military service in Sweden, he set off on his travels once more – this time to Africa.

He was twenty-one when he landed in Khartoum, continuing

from there to Eritrea and Ethiopia. The innocent abroad who had lost all his money almost before he had even set off was by now a seasoned globetrotter. In northern Ethiopia Stieg was interrogated by M.I.6, the British security service. In addition to being scared stiff and angry, he fell seriously ill after staying in a cheap hotel in Addis Ababa. For some considerable time he had no opportunity to contact anyone in Sweden, and it was not until he arrived in Kenya in a bus convoy that he could send a message confirming that he was O.K. From Kenya he continued on to Uganda, where he was able to catch a flight to Moscow, and from there back home to Sweden.

It wasn't the actual travelling that attracted him, though. More relevant was the fact that this way of gathering knowledge would help him to become what he now knew he wanted to be: a journalist. He had already made up his mind to enrol on a course in Stockholm. As if to mark the fact that this signalled a new phase in his life, he changed his first name.

That was when he became Stieg Larsson.

As with so much else in his life, his name change was something he preferred not to talk about, and he never told me exactly why he did it. Perhaps he was afraid that people would find it a bit odd. If there was anything he avoided like the plague, it was seeming to pretend to be somebody special.

Yet again I found myself asking myself the same old question: Who was Stieg?

I think the only answer that holds water is that he was a combination of the people who influenced his life, not least his grandfather Severin, his grandmother Tekla, his mother, Vivianne, his father, Erland, and his partner, Eva. But there was also an element of escapism. He was always aware of the need to keep pushing at the boundaries. He moved from Umeå to Stockholm. Took his typewriter and telescope with him. But he needed to keep pressing on. New goals, new challenges. The letter added to his first name fitted the pattern, because it also *hid* something. Stieg always kept something hidden, despite the fact that he invariably gave so much to everyone with whom he came into contact.

It suddenly occurs to me that it could well be this ability to hide things that made him unique as a writer of crime fiction. He had so many secrets – perhaps the most extreme example of that is the crime trilogy he wrote at night. Quite a lot of people knew that he was writing, and he also referred frequently to crime novels by other authors, claiming that he could write at least as well as they did. But that is not what I mean. The fact is that he wrote three thumping great novels before getting round to submitting them to a publisher. How common is that? Why did he do it? In so many ways, Stieg was and always will be an enigma. The bottom line is that part of his character was mysterious.

At the same time, few people are as generous in their relationships as Stieg was. He gave, and so many of us were keen to receive what he had to offer. I have no doubt at all how he would have responded to Raymond Carver's two momentous questions.

Did you get what you wanted from this life?
Yes.
And what did you want?
To be loved.

2

The first conversation

The most stereotyped crime novels generally begin with a telephone call. A chief inspector is woken up in the middle of the night by persistent ringing. Eventually he gropes sleepily for the receiver, checks the clock and is informed that a murder has been committed. He has to stagger out into the freezing-cold winter's night and make his way to the scene of the crime. The drama can begin.

It was not in the middle of the night that the story of Stieg and me began, but it did start with a telephone call. I still remember exactly when it was: Tuesday, 4 February, 1992. When I reached for the telephone, which was ringing just as persistently as in a sleepy chief inspector's bedroom, the voice I heard skipped the usual polite preliminaries: "I hope I'm not disturbing you at an inconvenient moment. I have something important to discuss."

At the time I was a member of the 21 February Committee and was sitting in their newly established headquarters in the Kungsholmen district of Stockholm. The committee's name referred to a strike that had been called in reaction to the shooting of eleven people in Stockholm by an individual the media had labelled the Laser Man. Hardly a day passed without the newspapers printing long articles about this lunatic who had been wandering around in broad daylight, aiming his laser sights at dark-skinned immigrants. The capital was on tenterhooks for several months, especially since one of the victims, a Swedish-

Iranian interpreter, had been shot dead on 8 November, 1991. Another ten immigrants had been seriously wounded, some of their injuries potentially fatal.

It would be no exaggeration to say that during these terrible months Stockholm felt like a city under siege. If not for all its citizens, then certainly for those with dark skins. It was a time many commentators called the most repugnant in recent Swedish history – a period full of menace and political betrayal.

I quickly realized that the caller had no intention of congratulating me on my role as a strike organizer. He continued without pausing: "You have said on the radio and television that if it were not for immigrants, Sweden would grind to a halt. You're absolutely right. But why is it only immigrants who are allowed to take part in the strike? What you have said excludes the majority of the population. How do you envisage including *my* solidarity with Swedish immigrants?"

"Er . . ." I began, but was immediately interrupted.

"I was born in Skellefteå of two Swedish parents, but I've lived for many years in the Stockholm suburb of Rinkeby, which has a high proportion of immigrant residents. I want to take part in the strike on 21 February, because racism isn't just an immigrant problem, it's a problem for Sweden as a whole."

Obviously, I understood what he was leading up to, but he didn't allow me to get a word in edgeways before making his own proposal.

"I want you to call a press conference and say that everybody in Sweden, irrespective of the colour of their skin, their gender, their mother tongue, their nationality, their homeland, their sexual orientation or their religion, is welcome to take part in this strike to demonstrate solidarity with immigrant Swedes at 10.00 this coming Friday."

Only then did he explain who he was. I recognized his name, having been present once or twice when he had delivered an address, usually at some demonstration or other, or at a rally to express solidarity with refugees. Most importantly, I knew he was the author of the pioneering book *Extremhögern*, an analysis of anti-democratic movements that had been published the previous year. It was a book I had been unable to put down.

Nevertheless I would be lying if I were to claim that I believed for one second that this telephone call was the beginning of a lifelong friendship.

Before we hung up – I had hardly said a word – he invited me to come and listen to his lecture "The Far Right in Sweden and Europe", to be delivered that same evening at the Swedish W.E.A. in Stockholm. I spent some considerable time wondering if there were any reasons why I shouldn't go.

I realized immediately that Stieg had put his finger on something important. Of course it was wrong to exclude anybody from a demonstration intended as an expression of frustration at feeling excluded. But it wasn't so easy to change such a significant decision – not when you had been voted into the office you held by 128 ethnic, anti-racist and religious associations and intercultural organizations all over Sweden. There were many different opinions to take into consideration. In such circumstances key decisions must be taken by a committee, which in this case comprised thirteen members with views that were often very different.

And time was short. All the leaflets and suchlike had already been ordered from the printer's and posters had even been sent to all the towns where rallies were to be held. Then had come that urgent telephone call to put the cat among the pigeons. I had no doubt that this Stieg Larsson was absolutely right, however. In a strange way I seemed to have known that all along: the telephone call was simply the catalyst that spurred me to do something about it.

I did what struck me as being the right thing to do: called my contact at Swedish Radio and announced that everybody in Sweden, irrespective of skin colour, gender, mother tongue, nationality, homeland, sexual orientation or religion, was welcome to take part in the demonstration, with the rallying call "Sweden will grind to a halt without immigrants."

Nine months passed between that telephone call and my first real meeting with Stieg. Not surprisingly, it took place over lunch. We arranged to meet at the modest Vasa restaurant in Odenplan, a mere stone's throw away from my office in Rehnsgatan.

This was before mobile phones had come into their own, enabling people to ring to say they had been delayed. I sat there wondering where he had got to. I did all the usual things – read a newspaper, thought about what else I had to do that day, made an occasional note in my diary. Then I looked at the clock for what must have been the hundredth time. Still no sign of Stieg. I'm usually pretty tolerant when it comes to people turning up late, but now I was starting to get annoyed. It was nearly an hour after the time we had agreed to meet and I found myself formulating a rather stiff dressing-down. I had better things to do than hang about in a third-rate restaurant all day. Besides, I was hungry. Now it was 2.00; if it hadn't been for my Kurdish upbringing I would no doubt have ordered food long since. To make matters worse, waiters were hovering around my table, as if they expected me to continue sitting there on my own, then leave without ordering anything. An hour and a quarter late, I thought to myself, smacking the table with my rolled-up newspaper. That's it. Enough is enough.

Just as I was getting up to leave, I noticed out of the corner of my eye a smiling, self-assured-seeming man wearing round glasses, a grey corduroy jacket, a checked shirt and a yellow polka-dot tie. He approached me at a leisurely pace, running his hand through his light brown hair. The first thing that struck me was that anybody observing this man would never have dreamt that he was over an hour late for an appointment.

"I'm sorry," he said as he sat down. "I've been held up by the usual threats. The police tell me I have to be careful. My way of dealing with this is never to turn up on time. Are you hungry? I only want a cup of coffee."

We shook hands; he lit a cigarette and leaned back in his chair.

"No problem," I said with a shrug. "Ever since I was a kid things have always gone wrong for me on Wednesdays. Why should today be any different?"

I was not happy with either my attempt to smooth things over or Stieg's evasive apology, but I did my best to conceal my irritation. I ordered cod and boiled potatoes, not expecting the food to put me in a better mood.

To begin with, we talked about *Svartvitt* (Black and White), the anti-racist magazine of which I was editor-in-chief. It had been launched as a not-for-profit venture on 20 October, 1987, the remit being to focus on matters of tolerance that other publications seemed to shy away from. Many critics regarded it as provocative. Stieg praised it to the skies. I liked the calm way in which he talked; his tone was warm and convincing, even if there was also something intriguing about it. At first I thought it was another of his precautionary measures, trying to seem a bit mysterious and elusive, at least when meeting face to face.

We moved on to the topics of the moment – the Laser Man, the way in which the populist protest party New Democracy had wormed its way into the parliament after the 1991 general election, the increasingly anti-immigrant image of the Sweden Democrats, and the incredibly naive reaction of the established parties to the threats to democracy these developments posed.

We must have talked for at least two hours. Ashtrays were changed regularly and rapidly filled by Stieg's cigarette butts. Despite the fact that we had only just met, it felt as if we had known each other for ages. I thought he was one of the most courageous people I had ever encountered. There was no mistaking his commitment – I had rarely come across anybody more passionately convinced of the democratic ideal and the equality of all human beings.

But at the same time there was something modest about him. I immediately detected a paradox in Stieg Larsson's make-up, and my suspicions would be confirmed as the years passed. He would go out of his way to find people with whom he could work, but all the while he wanted to dictate the way in which the cooperation functioned. He disliked being in the limelight and doing all the talking, especially on television. This led to friction at times, and when I look back over the years we worked together, this contradiction was nearly always the root cause of our disagreements.

Having said that, the paradox was convincingly trumped by the vehemence he displayed in his fight against racism and neo-Nazism. It is simply impossible to describe how passionate, how fervent, not to say how obsessed he was by this mission. I once described him as a mixture of Malcolm X, Martin Luther King, the Dalai Lama and Pippi Longstocking. I concede that this was perhaps a little crude, but it was a sincere attempt to pin down a man with unique and contradictory character traits of a type one rarely encounters.

Another thing that struck me that first time we sat talking – me waiting for my lunch, Stieg with his cups of coffee and his cigarettes – was how animatedly he gesticulated. He also impressed me with the breadth and depth of his knowledge. Naturally, we were well aware that the precarious position in which Sweden found itself in 1992 was nothing compared with the intolerant, anti-immigrant forces at work in Denmark, Holland, Switzerland, Norway, Belgium and Italy. We were indisputably living in a Europe beginning to show its claws in a way that made us worry that a catastrophe might be imminent.

You could say that Sweden was emerging from a Sleeping Beauty-like torpor. For years Swedes had been convinced that they were immune from racism – not the unease with regard to everything new and foreign that is sometimes discussed around dinner tables here and there, but the *organized* antipathy that arranges demonstrations at election meetings and tries to influence decisions made at local, regional and central government level. During our lunch Stieg compared these forces to a virus spreading through Sweden. He maintained that the battle against them needed fighting every day. If one ignored the situation for long enough, it could become an uncontrolled epidemic.

I have often been accused of being a bad listener. People tell me I talk too much. No doubt they are right. But on that occasion I hardly said a word; I sat there entranced by Stieg's powerful imagery, neat turns of phrase and black humour. Believe it or not, I let him say all he had to say without interruption. Perhaps I was already fascinated by the contradictory nature of what he was saying. In addition to the mixture of team player and solo performer already mentioned, there was also a remarkable combination of stress and inner calm. He spoke both forcefully and calmly about important principles: about how people should never be insulted, about the struggle for women's rights, about the importance of humane refugee policies. Matters that most people would agree on, even if many would nod in approval but not do very much about ensuring that things changed for the better. Here was a man who would never give up until the goals had been achieved.

Stieg's duality was a feature of our friendship from the very start. But there was no question at all about where his heart was. During all the years of our friendship I never doubted for one single second that Stieg Larsson was on the side of the weak and vulnerable. He was always prepared to speak up for anybody and everybody incapable of making a case for themselves. And that was not all: he was willing to pay a high price in order to bring about change.

I had realized this long before the sad-looking cod and over-cooked potatoes landed on the table with a thud.

*

How can you get to know somebody who hardly ever talks about his private life? That's something I've often thought about. Whenever Stieg entered a room, he automatically became the centre of attention. Despite that, it was impossible to regard him as anything other than unpretentious.

Some people would no doubt maintain that the fact he spoke so little about himself and was always keen to avoid the limelight was due to his northern Swedish origins. He often reminded people that he was, for better or worse, from the far north. He actually said as much the very first time we spoke, during that brief telephone call. He referred to his northern origins and the fact that he had been involved in politics while still clinging to his mother's apron strings – those two basic facts about Stieg are impossible to ignore.

You may be born a northerner, but being involved in politics is something else entirely. Stieg's burning interest in politics was aroused as early as 1968, when he was fourteen years old. He was lucky in that his mother, Vivianne, was devoid of prejudice and loved to indulge in long political discussions. He spent hours talking to her about starvation in Biafra, Soviet aggression or the Vietnam War – much of his passion for justice can doubtless be traced back to conversations with his mother in their kitchen. Contemporaries also attest that Stieg's mother was a gifted story-teller; perhaps he learned a few tricks from her, who knows?

The 1970s were a politically charged decade, and Stieg was hardly the only fourteen-year-old to protest against the Vietnam War by joining the National Liberation Front. Even at secondary school he contributed polemical articles to newspapers and magazines.

Nevertheless, his political involvement cannot be explained exclusively by the trends of the time or some kind of teenage revolt. It was a built-in part of his character, just like his northern origins.

There are few aspects of my life that cannot be traced back to the fact that I am a Kurd. The inevitability of my being an outsider is obviously associated with my origins. I am closely linked with a people that is either disowned or opposed. This fact is an important part of my make-up and my memories, and it has inevitably formed what interests and drives me.

But the feeling of being an outsider can manifest itself in many different ways. There is no doubt that Stieg also felt that he was excluded. In his case it was due largely to his working-class background, but also to his political sympathies. I think this is why he never went to university and instead built his career on his trade union activities. A characteristic of trade unionists is that they often work full-time during the day in order to earn a living, devoting themselves to the things that really interest them – together with others similarly minded – in their spare time. Perhaps this doesn't apply to everybody, but it certainly applied to Stieg. He went out of his way to ensure that he always had a secure job, and after an eight-hour working day he would turn his full attention to anti-racist activities.

The project he was most proud of was his contribution as Nordic correspondent to the British magazine *Searchlight*. He often told me about his assignments in Grenada and Eritrea. In a way, perhaps, it was revenge for being rejected by the Stockholm

College of Journalism on the grounds that his school leaving grades were not good enough. We had been friends for a long time before I heard about that. I tried to imagine how Stieg must have felt. He was passionate about writing on important matters and knew he could do it as well as anybody; but he failed to gain a place on a course which would have made things easier for him in many ways – work experience posts on a variety of newspapers, opportunities to build up a network of contacts while being trained.

What did it feel like for a working-class boy from the remote north of Sweden to find the door slammed in his face? I think it was a setback that scarred Stieg for life. He once told me in confidence that if there was one person he admired, it was his grandfather Severin Boström, for his determined opposition to Hitler during the Second World War – activities that continued long after the peace treaty was signed in 1945. Perhaps it was his grandfather who was the inspiration for Stieg's education in the university of life, far from Stockholm and academia, and who convinced him that a man can achieve a lot if he is passionate about a cause.

3

Expo – blowing the whistle on extremism

Baobab trees thrive best on the savannah, where they tower majestically over the flat grassland. The branches are magnificent, but look a bit awkward compared with the enormous trunks. A baobab tree needs well-drained soil and is unique in that it can suck up such a large amount of water that it survives even long periods of drought. But it is extremely sensitive to rot and dislikes the cold. It is also known as the monkey-bread tree, after its pear-like fruits. Presumably monkeys are especially fond of them.

If you glance quickly at a baobab tree, it almost looks as if it is growing upside down. A substantial trunk some twenty metres tall, with a small crown at the top. It is hardly surprising that there are many folktales and legends about the baobab. Most of them claim that a god became so angry with the tree that he pulled it up, roots and all, then replanted it with the branches downwards.

I sometimes suggest that idealistic, not-for-profit magazines are like the baobab tree. The difference is that magazines suck up money rather than water. But what decides whether a magazine will survive or not is how long it can keep going during long periods of drought.

Without a doubt, the most important project in Stieg's life was the magazine *Expo*, which he and others founded as a result of his belief that it was essential to create a Swedish version of *Searchlight*. His view was hardly surprising: the situation in Sweden was deteriorating in a worrying way. In the 1994 elections, the Sweden Democrats polled almost fourteen thousand votes, which gave them five seats on local councils. In 1988 they had received 1,118 votes and in 1991 4,887. In other words, they were expanding quickly – disturbingly quickly. In 1991 they had won two local council seats without causing much of a reaction.

The established parliamentary parties were not at all sure how to deal with the situation and tended to wash their hands of it, treating it as an aberration. But it turned out to be an aberration that developed into something much bigger. In the 2006 elections the Sweden Democrats got 162,463 votes and won 281 local council seats. This boil on the skin of Swedish democracy was the main reason why *Expo* came into existence.

During the years it took to build *Expo* up from nothing, Stieg had to endure his fair share of successes and droughts. I was able to observe his indefatigability over and over again. Sometimes I am convinced that *Expo* cut Stieg's life short, because of all the threats it received and the financial crises it suffered. Other times I have the feeling that it was thanks to *Expo* that Stieg was able to find the space his creativity needed – it was almost as if it provided the air he required in order to breathe.

Stieg's relationship with *Expo* – it really is possible to see it as a relationship between two people – was filled with happiness, creativity, setbacks and complications. Not least with love. The staff were a collection of young and hungry journalists keen to face up to big challenges. Stieg stood out for many reasons, one being his experience – in the mid-1980s he was among those who launched the anti-violence project Stop Racism. Moreover, he was the only one at the magazine over thirty.

Starting something from nothing has advantages and disadvantages. It can be time-consuming to procure the resources necessary to make a project happen, but it is also stimulating to realize exactly what you have envisaged. Along with the others, Stieg threw himself wholeheartedly into *Expo*. There were big problems to solve and minor matters to sort out – the bottom line was that everything needed to be resolved in the shortest possible time.

The first matter to be tackled was ownership. The first owner was the Hill Foundation, which eventually became the *Expo* Research Foundation. Next, *Expo*'s remit was spelled out:

> . . . to study and survey anti-democratic, right-wing extremist and racist tendencies in Swedish society. All activities are idealistic and non-profit-making. The foundation's policy is to safeguard democracy and freedom of expression against racist, right-wing extremist, anti-Semitic and totalitarian tendencies in society. *Expo* has no links to specific parties or political groups, but cooperates with all individuals and groups that share the foundation's philosophy.

A lot of effort went into raising the necessary capital, not least in order to begin the intensive work on creating an international archive comprising thousands of books, posters, magazines, newspaper articles, videos, records and photographs linked in one way or another to racism, neo-Nazism and far-right extremism. The archive soon became unique and irreplaceable. There was only one problem: the costs had got out of hand.

Expo moved first into basement premises in Lundagatan in

the Södra district of Stockholm (Lisbeth Salander's first flat was located in the very same street); by the end of 1995 they had moved to a cheaper basement at Färggårdstorget 32, in the Skanstull district. That same year saw the publication of the first issue. One of the pictures in it showed a person giving the Nazi salute, but hiding his face behind a partially open door.

The editorial board could not possibly have imagined the success they went on to achieve with their first thirty-two pages. Stieg wrote the leading article about the horrific bomb outrage in Oklahoma City in April 1995, which cost 168 lives. The board was delighted to note that the matters they took up in that first issue were being discussed in lively debates in schools and workplaces, by trade unions and political parties.

The journal immediately attracted large numbers of subscribers, several of whom paid more than the nominal fee in order to demonstrate their support. But there were also critical voices. Some commentators felt that *Expo* had acted in an unethical way and gone too far in its efforts to track down racist networks. Every journal with high ideals can expect criticism; much worse were the constant threats. Needless to say, a magazine that devotes so much effort to identifying racist and neo-Nazi activities will create enemies. The last thing people involved in such activities want is to find themselves in the spotlight. And they think nothing of resorting to violent tactics.

From the very start *Expo*'s staff were labelled as "traitors" in neo-Nazi publications, and countless defamatory letters were sent to newspaper editors and to parliamentary parties and their youth sections. The first organized hate campaign took place in May of 1996 – fifteen months after *Expo*'s launch – when the magazine's printer's premises were sabotaged. Every window was smashed and totally demolished using glass-cutters, in order to demonstrate how easily the building could be entered if the firm continued to print *Expo*. Retailers offering *Expo* for sale suffered similar attacks and walls were sprayed with the message "Don't Print *Expo*!"

Of course, attacks of this kind often have a positive side: they set people talking. The subsequent debate means that editors and commentators are forced to take sides, and that in turn leads to discussion points rising to the surface. Very few people want to live in a society where you put your life in danger by printing a magazine.

In any case, it was obvious that a lot of people were actually jealous of all the attention *Expo* had been lucky enough to attract in such a short time. Some commentators stood the situation on its head and wondered how much support a right-wing-extremist equivalent of *Expo* would receive if it suffered a similar attack. *Expo*'s new editor-in-chief, Andreas Rosenlund, made several brilliant contributions to the debate that followed. He summarized the situation by pointing out that "instead of trying to conduct a democratic exchange of views, these people turn to gangster tactics".

Despite all the support the journal received during these difficult weeks, nobody was able to convince the printers that it was a price worth paying for freedom of speech. They had been so scared that they felt obliged to cancel their contract with *Expo*.

It was not necessary to call in a world-class sleuth in order to work out who was behind the campaign of violence directed at retailers selling *Expo*. The neo-Nazi newspaper *Info-14* – which, remarkably enough, produced its first edition the same year, 1995 – reported promptly and in detail on how the attacks had been carried out, going so far as to propose new targets. As well as being a newspaper, *Info-14* was a political outlet for the National Alliance. Its founder, Robert Vesterlund, was also chairman of Sweden Democratic Youth. The police interrogated large numbers of people associated with the newspaper, but never managed to bring anybody to trial.

As so often happens, the racist attacks had the opposite effect to what had been intended. On 10 June, 1996, the editorial boards of Sweden's two biggest evening newspapers, *Aftonbladet* and *Expressen*, decided to demonstrate their solidarity with *Expo* by publishing and distributing without charge an edition of the journal together with one of their own issues, with a print run of over eight hundred thousand.

Expo's list of subscribers increased significantly, and the smile on Stieg's lips became broader than ever. He even plucked up enough courage to joke about the thugs threatening him, calling them his "prey". They consisted of a motley collection of latent neo-Nazis in Strängnäs, active neo-Nazis and members of the National Socialist Front in Skåne, and lunatics in the Keep Sweden Swedish organization in Uppsala, Västerås and Helsingborg. Several of them were subscribers, even though their motivation had nothing to do with boosting *Expo*'s finances. They would open each new issue in a state of expectancy: would fingers be pointed at them in one of the articles? Some of them considered it a significant milestone in their careers as racists, being mentioned by name in *Expo*. No doubt many of them were excused from paying for a round or two of beer in pubs in Skåne and Östgötaland as a result.

Sad to say, however, the attacks on printing works and retail outlets were only the beginning. It was not long before worse atrocities took place, often in Stieg's and my backyard. I am sometimes shattered by memories of what happened in those days.

A cursory glance at press cuttings from the time reveals a remarkable phenomenon. Quite a lot of people in Sweden are murdered by neo-Nazis shortly after parliamentary elections. According to statistics, the year after an election can be critical for people who don't "look Swedish" and who have names that are difficult to pronounce, Swedish anti-racists, anybody who has adopted a non-Scandinavian child, local politicians and journalists who expose racist tendencies.

Of all the horrific racist outrages, one stands out. It took place on 16 August, 1995, at Lake Ingetorp in Kode, near Gothenburg. A fourteen-year-old boy, John Hron, had gone there camping with a friend. They had been looking forward to this outing, but the situation changed drastically when four young neo-Nazis turned up. The two boys were subjected to psychological and physical torture for three hours. John escaped by swimming out into the lake, but was forced to return when the neo-Nazis threatened to kill his friend. He swam back, at which point they turned their full attention on him. Having allowed his friend to escape, they subjected John to sophisticated torture: they would beat and kick him for a while, then change tactics and speak nicely to him, offering him a beer. In the end, having rendered him unconscious, they threw him into the water and watched him drown.

How can one explain such unprovoked violence? Is it possible to understand such bestial treatment simply because somebody has a foreign-sounding name?

The next victim of racist violence was Patrick Nadji, an asylum-seeker from the Ivory Coast. Two young neo-Nazis stabbed Patrick to death in Klippan, in Skåne. Why? "Because," according to the murderers, "he was a nigger." Moreover, the young man wielding the knife considered himself to be innocent: "I didn't do nothing. The nigger just jumped on to my knife."

It is one thing to associate neo-Nazi crimes with disaffected young people – it is no doubt possible to find all sorts of extenuating circumstances. But nobody should imagine that these were simply cases of isolated individuals acting out their fantasies about national superiority, ethnic cleansing and their other twisted ideologies. *Expo* was not content with exposing them as individuals. More important was the fact that there was increasing support for xenophobic tendencies in Swedish society. That was the root cause of the increase in hate crimes.

Despite *Expo*'s many sympathizers, problems soon started piling up. As the threats increased, advertising decreased. The number of subscribers sank steadily towards a thousand – the goal originally had been five thousand, but even when the journal was enjoying its greatest success, in the spring of 1996, the number was no more than two thousand.

In addition, one of the journal's staff stole 50,000 kronor from the sparse kitty because, as he put it, he needed money "to pick up women at Café Opera". To crown it all, a serious credibility problem arose when it was disclosed that one of *Expo*'s researchers had been reported to the police for criminal damage.

But the most serious threat to *Expo*'s existence was that there were too many colleagues pulling in different directions. Everybody worked almost 24/7. They woke up to *Expo* and dreamt of *Expo*. There was no time to stop and think; all that mattered was hard work, generally unpaid. There came a point when Stieg demanded even more sacrifices, but his colleagues felt they had given up enough of their time and their private lives. His solution was to work even harder. Everybody was aware of his inexhaustible capacity for work. The problem was that he demanded just as much of his colleagues as he did from himself.

Despite the enormous amount of work put into it, the journal found itself teetering on the brink of bankruptcy. In the end it was obvious to everybody that even Stieg was under extreme pressure. He seemed more and more worried, and his smile became increasingly strained. The prophets of doom were only too ready to put the boot in. They said Stieg was not cut out to be a manager, that he was a catastrophe as an administrator and financial officer. In many ways they were right. Stieg was fantastic with language, but only human (to say the least) when it came to figures and statistics. He was driven by the conviction that Sweden required a journal to keep an eye on anti-democratic developments. In order to produce one, he needed a closely knit team to work tirelessly on an idealistic basis for little financial reward.

That was when everything unravelled. Several contributors resigned from the editorial board, which in turn meant that those who stayed on had to work even harder. Stieg never really forgave the ones who left, even though he must have realized that, less than three years after its launch, *Expo* was about to sink.

During 1996 and 1997 the editorial board could have been compared to a football team. It comprised Stieg, Andreas, Jenny, Emmy, Tobias, Katarina, Peter, David, Micael, Mikael and a graphic designer. Stieg began as goalkeeper, in order to have the best possible overall view. But as colleagues resigned he also became team captain. That wasn't enough. So he decided to become the team's trainer as well. That wasn't enough either, because he was forced to accept the fact that the number of players at his disposal was becoming fewer and fewer. Having urged them to take the field for one final effort, he asked the referee for extra time.

Stieg refused to let *Expo* die. The idea that it was over and done for was not something that he could possibly contemplate. This despite the fact that it was clear to any objective observer that the journal was beyond help. Little did I think that I would play a leading role in the reincarnation of *Expo* lurking round the corner.

I knew that Stieg was under extreme pressure. It was obvious that *Expo*'s misfortunes were taking their toll. We had been meeting regularly for some years and regarded each other as close friends. He called me his kid brother and I called him my big brother. At first it was mainly for fun, but as time passed the names became a true reflection of our mutual trust.

One day in May 1998, we were in one of Stieg's favourite cafés, Il Caffè in Kungsholmen, and I had barely taken my first sip of coffee before it became clear that he had something important on his mind.

"Do you realize that I have very few real friends?"

Shaking my head, I said, "Perhaps you work too hard. Friends demand time, we both know that."

He agreed, and looked sad, almost dejected, which was very unlike him.

"*Expo* is in ruins," he said, looking down at his feet.

"So I've gathered."

"We haven't been able to do any proper journalism for ages. But we do have a trump card – our archive on neo-Nazism and racism in Europe."

Then something remarkable happened. It was as if at that very moment Stieg began to relive everything the journal had achieved, as if the solution to all its problems had suddenly dawned on him. Presumably he had already decided what he was going to do, but he gave the impression that it was happening even as he spoke, as if his words were leading him on. It was almost as if this was the moment when he regained his faith in *Expo*. As if an idea had just struck like a flash of lightning and taken possession of him.

"It's time to take some decisions," he said, leaning back in the little chair at the rear of the café. "I've been looking for a collaborator who will allow *Expo* to go its own way. I want to work with a journal without links to any particular political party. I'm tired of people accusing us of being a journal linked to the left."

Then he leaned forward and looked me in the eye.

"I'll come clean. We have about sixty kronor in the kitty. Do you think you could come to *Expo*'s rescue?"

I sat there in astonishment.

"How do you think that would be possible?"

"I thought you'd ask that," he said, stubbing out his cigarette. The smile I was so familiar with returned to his face, those sparkling eyes and the gesticulating hands. "I want *Expo* and *Svartvitt* to join forces. *Expo* will be a financial burden, but you'll earn a lot of goodwill. Besides, I'm convinced that you will be rewarded some time in the future."

I couldn't help laughing at such an optimistic prophesy, but Stieg merely brushed my laughter aside and continued.

"Now to the nitty-gritty. I want you to fund the printing and distribution of *Expo*. I'll take care of the editorial side. *Svartvitt*'s editorial staff are experienced in administering and funding a magazine. My colleagues and I are good at research and journalism, but we don't seem to be much good at anything else."

I leaned back in my chair and wondered what on earth to say. I had thought we were going to have a cup of coffee and chat like we usually did. Now I found myself faced with a proposal to merge our journals.

I said nothing for quite a while. I agreed totally with Stieg that our publications had a lot in common. Unfortunately the financial state of both operations was also more similar than he seemed to realize. The National Council for Cultural Affairs had just cut *Svartvitt*'s grant to 30,000 kronor. I had been so angry that I had called it "pin money", or so some cultural journalists had claimed. In order to make a point I had rejected the grant altogether. To make matters worse, we had just moved into larger premises in Pilgatan. You could hardly say that *Svartvitt* was in a fit state to take on new costs.

"I agree with you," I said in the end. "*Expo* is too important to be allowed to collapse. I'm prepared to do my bit. But how will it be done, in practical terms? Shall we have two publishers and two editors-in-chief?"

"I thought *Expo*'s pages should be yellow instead of white. We'll design and produce between twelve and twenty-four pages. You'll pay for the printing and distribution. You can be editor-in-chief of both *Svartvitt* and *Expo*. Somebody from *Expo* can be the publisher. That way you can escape being taken to court all the time."

We both laughed at that. Stieg continued talking. He seemed to be in an exalted state now, gesticulating more and more wildly, with increasing confidence. I had swallowed the bait, and he knew it.

"Behind closed doors I will be the editor, but I don't want my name linked publicly with the job."

"As usual, in other words," I said.

"*Expo* and *Svartvitt* will be two independent and equal journals. None of us will have the right to interfere in the editorial work of the other. Is that sufficiently clear?"

"How long have you been thinking about this?"

He smiled and shrugged.

"Maybe I just thought it up."

"That wouldn't surprise me," I said. "But I have a few questions, Stieg. How come *Expo* writes so much about equality, but behaves like a men's club? How can an anti-racist journal find it so difficult to recruit staff with an immigrant background?"

"I agree. We lack credibility in that respect. We must do something about it immediately."

"O.K.," I said. "Those are my only objections. We can publish our journals jointly – let's say until the next election. Then we'll have to take stock and decide if we should continue. But before we shake hands on it, I want to propose a better deal than the one you offered me. We'll pay for printing and distribution. Can you pay the rent? If we make a profit, which I don't suppose we shall, we'll share the profits. If we run at a loss, I'll be responsible for the entire amount."

When we shook hands Stieg smiled more broadly than I had ever seen him do before. Although in fact he seemed more relieved than happy. It was as if a burden had been lifted from his shoulders. Perhaps he wasn't convinced that he had saved *Expo*, but he was pretty sure that he had bought enough time to ride out the storm.

"On Monday," I said, raising my coffee cup as if in a toast, "I'll arrange for a contract to be drawn up that both parties can sign. We can't have any misunderstandings just because you and I are such good friends."

He looked hard at me, then rolled another cigarette and lifted a yellow lighter with his left hand.

"No, Kurdo," he said rather sternly. "We don't need a contract. If I didn't trust you I would never have contacted you in the first place. I know you won't let me down. An oral promise and a handshake will be sufficient. From January onwards we'll publish *Svartvitt* together with *Expo*. We'll take care of the rent."

"O.K."

"What do you say to announcing the merger of Sweden's two most important anti-racist journals on 30 November?"

"That sounds like an excellent idea," I said, realizing that this was something he'd been thinking about in order to attract maximum publicity. It was also practical to supply our combined subscribers with the news about *Svartvitt* and *Expo* on the day when nationalists celebrate the exploits of the Swedish warrior-king Charles XII. (Why they should want to do that is a bit of a mystery, as his defeat in the Great Northern War effectively brought the Swedish Empire to an end.)

We said goodbye outside Tidningarnas Telegrambyrå, headquarters of the Swedish Central News Agency, in Scheelegatan. I watched Stieg vanish through the door and found myself thinking about the remarkable baobab tree. For eleven years I had been carefully tending my own little tree known as *Svartvitt*. It was clear that I was now faced with a major challenge.

I eventually decided that two trees with similar characteristics would be bound to thrive together. They could support and shade each other in difficult times, which ought to make it easier for both to survive in the barren savannah. I felt happy and contented as I slowly made my way back to my office.

4

Stieg as colleague and journalist

I've suddenly remembered something that happened in the early hours of 9 November, 1999. I was staying at the Prize Hotel in Stockholm. The telephone rang at 2.15. Although I was still awake, alarm bells went off inside my head – one seldom receives good news in the middle of the night.

"Stieg hasn't come home," Eva screamed into my mobile.

She was sniffling and sobbing. I tried to calm her down, but I could feel myself going ice cold. In as soothing a voice as I could manage, I assured her that nothing bad could have happened. A few hours later it became apparent that Stieg had fallen asleep in his office. Probably, now that I think about it, he had been working and had decided, unusually, to lie down on a sofa.

Today, so many years later, I can laugh at the memory.

Was that the moment I realized that Stieg was writing books at night? I can't remember. But I do remember clearly how relieved I was that nothing awful had happened to him.

When Stieg was appointed to a post as a graphic designer at Tidningarnas Telegrambyrå, he could hardly have realized how long he would be associated with that place of work. Although he maintained throughout those years that T.T. played an important role in independent news-reporting, he had a remarkable love–hate relationship with it. No doubt his appointment was in many ways a sort of revenge as far as he was concerned. Now he could make up for the frustration he had felt on being rejected as an eighteen-year-old by the Stockholm College of Journalism in the autumn of 1972. Now he would show them that their idiotic admissions requirements meant they had lost a reporter who was more than a match for anybody.

It was this lust for revenge which ensured that he had a plan even when he walked for the first time through the door of the Hötorget skyscraper where T.T. was based in the 1970s. He would work at everything he was required to do in the way of illustrations, diagrams, pictures and paste-ups in order to become a fully fledged, damned good reporter in due course.

Things did not go according to plan, however. He was never given the assignments he expected, and the management appeared to have no interest at all in his ideas.

Despite this, T.T. came to mean an awful lot to Stieg. It was not simply a matter of earning a living, it was more a question of living or not living. The reasons why he could never bring himself to leave T.T. were mental, not financial.

I have worked through T.T.'s digital archives in an attempt to track down Stieg's articles. The first time his name crops up is in January 1982. On 11 July, 1985, his initials – "SLA" – appear in print for the first time. In connection with an illustration. Then follow hundreds of illustrations, diagrams, pictures and paste-ups, all signed by him. Strikingly often they are linked with financial articles.

The first article he wrote dates from 22 January, 1992, and is about the history of the Swedish intelligence agency. If you consider all the years Stieg worked at T.T., he wrote comparatively few articles of any length. I have traced twenty-five written between 1992 and 1999. Eight are tips for crime novels to read at

Christmas or during the summer holidays, which is interesting in view of what happened later. The articles show clearly that Stieg was impressed by the novels of Sara Paretsky, Harlan Ellison, Liza Cody and, last but by no means least, Elizabeth George.

Nevertheless, most of the articles are in his field of expertise: neo-Nazism and racism in Sweden and abroad. Three of them are about the bomb outrage in Oklahoma. Of course, there may be many more unsigned articles by Stieg, and one cannot exclude the possibility that several signed articles were overlooked during the scanning process (those who worked on it have admitted that T.T.'s repository of news articles is far from complete).

So, although he was fighting against the odds, Stieg hung on at T.T. He was pretty frank about his conviction that obstacles were constantly being placed in his way, not least because his superiors seldom allowed him to write about matters on which he was an expert. Nevertheless he never felt for one second that he was being victimized. Instead, he mounted counterattacks whenever opportunities presented themselves. He even went so far as to organize his own "resistance group" at T.T. This included several members of staff who got on well together and had more or less the same views on journalism. This group supported him when his superiors complained or prevaricated.

Now, many years later, I find it hard to understand why he behaved as he did. Why this constant battle? Couldn't he have done what everybody else would have done and simply looked for another job? Sometimes I suspect he liked to create his own battlefield where he could leap up on to his horse and wield his sword and bayonet. The image of Don Quixote occasionally crops up in my mind's eye.

Similarly, T.T. seems like a big windmill spinning round at a leisurely pace. Or perhaps a fan belt whizzing round out of sight inside an engine which ought to be changed after a certain number of kilometres but is still there. You almost get the feeling that the whole engine will grind to a halt when the belt eventually snaps. It often seemed as if those in charge at T.T. had no idea how to handle the bolshie employee from the far north who was at one moment an implacable warhorse and at the next moment more like a miserable schoolboy sulking in a corner of the playground. They never knew if he was going to do his own thing – and ignore their rules – or toe the line.

There is no point in suppressing the fact that on occasion Stieg stretched the rules to breaking point. For instance, as a T.T. reporter he wrote news items about having himself received death threats. Nobody at T.T. seems to have noticed. Or possibly they didn't have the strength to argue with him and so turned a blind eye. A quick glance at T.T.'s archives shows that in his capacity as a member of the *Expo* editorial board, he "interviewed" himself five times in the period 1992–9.

It was precisely this lack of impartiality and relevance that made his position at T.T. so complicated. Such goings-on are far removed from what a news agency ought to be doing. But Stieg simply couldn't help himself. The moment he sat down at a computer, he took sides for or against.

These facts make it easy to understand how *Expo* could have become such an important part of Stieg's life. The number of articles he wrote for T.T. declined in inverse proportion to his increasing involvement with *Expo*. Perhaps, paradoxically, this was what forced him to stay on at T.T. He needed his salaried post because *Expo*'s financial situation was always so awful.

Early on in our friendship I realized what the force was that drove Stieg: justice – irrespective of class, gender, ethnicity or sexual orientation. I couldn't possibly count how many times he said "Everybody is worth the same as everybody else." Over and over again. Most of us would agree, no doubt; but I have never heard that sentiment expressed with such emphasis and conviction. The concept of justice was an integral part of his being, I don't know how else to describe it.

Like many others of his generation, Stieg had grown up with a political vision, in his case Trotskyism. But unlike quite a few of his generation, he never changed his views when money was involved. Financial matters simply did not exist in his conception of the world; he had zero interest in anything to do with money.

More important to him was the possibility of making a difference without being noticed. That is why it is extremely difficult to imagine how he would have handled his success as an author, forced to take a bow because of all the attention his novels had attracted. But he was a man who worked tirelessly to produce material for the rest of us to present to the general public. A man who wrote vast numbers of appeals and articles, and then asked me to attach my name to them.

I know that he thought about this because he had premonitions that the Millennium trilogy would be a success. However, for me – and for many others – the biggest question is not how he would have handled his success, but how on earth he managed to produce these books in more or less total secrecy, despite being so busy all the time.

I sometimes ask myself just how much Stieg worked. I generally answer, "I can't say when he worked – but I can tell you when he *didn't* work. When he was asleep." I should perhaps mention that when he was not at the office, he was glued to his computer or had his mobile-clamped to his ear – two indefatigable "collaborators" of Stieg's.

When the time came for the first double edition of *Svartvitt* and *Expo*, Stieg had an unusually number of irons in the fire. He was fully occupied with contacting the parents of children who had been exposed to racist violence and with trying to find homes for women who had fled sects or families where they had been living under duress. He was also working intensively to arrange residence permits for homosexuals from Muslim backgrounds. He was helping others to finish books when they got stuck and couldn't make progress. He was lecturing regularly to Swedish PEN, the Helsinki Committee and Scotland Yard. In addition to all that was the non-stop fund-raising for victims of racism.

Moreover, Stieg had started digging into an old legal case that later came to be called the Joy Rahman affair and that led to Rahman being released from prison in 2002 and awarded substantial damages. Rahman, employed as a home help, had been sentenced to life imprisonment in 1994 for strangling a 72-year-old woman she had been working for in southern Stockholm. Stieg was convinced that Rahman was innocent, despite the fact that the Supreme Court had rejected her appeal. He thought that as a journalist I ought to be able to establish Rahman's innocence simply by reading all the legal documents carefully. He had dumped over a thousand pages of proceedings on my desk. I read all of them, but was not convinced that

Rahman had been falsely accused. Stieg disputed my conclusion.

"You're not going to win the major journalism prize," he said.

But I couldn't bring myself to query the legal process. There were too many details that seemed not to fit and far too many uncertainties. In 2007 the same Joy Rahman was imprisoned for the murder of a man in Bangladesh. I wonder what Stieg would have made of that.

Despite Stieg's enormous workload, he always met his deadlines. He never failed to complete a text by the time it was needed. Mind you, whether the article was what had been agreed in the first place was another matter.

Time was beginning to run out for our first combined issue. It was to contain no more than eight *Expo* pages: a single-column leader, four news reports, a commentary and a review. Stieg's article was still outstanding, and was essential if everything was to fit together with the *Svartvitt* material. That is what we had agreed, and it was important that nothing went wrong. We had too many critics just waiting to pounce if we made a mess of things. And we were in desperate need of new subscribers. In no circumstances must we publish late and give the impression of being unprofessional.

When Stieg turned up at the editorial office just inside the deadline with his article, I quickly realized that it was not what we had agreed on. It was in fact a book, forty pages long, entitled Euro-Nat – A Europe for Anti-Semites, Ethnic Warriors and Political Crackpots – The Sweden Democrats' International Network .

"It's urgent," he said. "Can you publish it?"

"I'll read it by tomorrow."

"No, you must read it now, right away."

"But I have to make sure we don't find ourselves with all sorts of legal problems. We can't afford that."

"You don't need to worry. The only people I've named fully are elected officials. All the others are referred to only by their first names. You're not risking anything. Can you give me an ISBN number from your *Svartvitt* list?"

I took a deep breath, closed my eyes and got up to fetch the list. It did occur to me that the book would be an excellent introduction to the partnership between *Svartvitt* and *Expo*.

In other words, I found myself becoming the publisher of a book I had never read. This was a reflection of how much confidence I had in Stieg. If he said that the book was important and there were no potential legal problems, I trusted him. The first thing I saw on my desk after his death was a copy of the jacket blurb for that book. It reminded me of the meeting I have just described. Stieg had written the text himself:

> In the 1998 elections the Sweden Democrats polled twenty thousand votes and won eight local council seats. That meant they were the third-largest party with no representation in the national parliament, and now they are setting their sights on the 1999 E.U. elections. They hope to hoover up votes from New Democracy, which has collapsed, and from other protest parties. The keyword in the Sweden Democrats' campaign is "respectability". This spruced-up façade is in stark contrast with the party's history, and its membership of the international movements Nord-Nat and Euro-Nat.

There was undeniably something electric about Stieg's

presence. If you managed to interpret the signals he sent out correctly, your whole environment was lit up. But if you misunderstood his intentions, he could burn everything that got in his way – including himself. So he was both a dream and a nightmare to work with. He was not merely seriously involved, but rather obsessed with the struggle to overcome intolerance. And he always acted spontaneously. When one least expected it, he was apt to come out with long quotations in order to illustrate his arguments. A lot of people called him un-Swedish, but I have never been able to accept that. It simply doesn't fit comfortably with his view of the world.

Every time I think about our meetings, it strikes me that some people might think that our contact was always linked with the work we did together. I have never seen it like that. It was about as far away from a working relationship as it's possible to get. It would be truer to say that our work was a part of our friendship.

On 30 November, 1998, T.T. issued a newsflash. The anti-racist journal *Expo* had been resurrected, thanks to a merger with the magazine *Svartvitt*.

I was quoted: "*Expo* has been outstandingly good at investigating racism, but they have never grasped how to make money. That is where I can help them."

According to the newsflash, the new version of *Expo* hoped to sell four thousand copies to start with and eventually nine thousand. Stieg was the main protagonist at the press conference held at the Swedish W.E.A. that same day. He was wearing his now legendary grey jacket and shirt with a dark blue tie. But the resulting news item didn't even mention his name: although he did most of the talking at the press conference, I was the one who was quoted. There again, I was the one at whom several people laughed when they heard the number of copies *Expo* hoped to sell. Nobody thought it was possible to achieve that ambition.

It was not only because of his shyness that Stieg maintained such a modest profile. His relationship with T.T. had reached a new low and he felt stymied. Because of his permanent post there, he was not free to be interviewed as an expert on matters involving racism or neo-Nazism. Nor was he allowed to write on these subjects. He was always being approached for articles that would have been right up his street. Sometimes he paid no attention to what his superiors said and wrote them. But that only made his position even more awkward.

You can't serve two masters, Stieg!

You simply can't do this.

You can't publish a journal about right-wing extremism in your spare time and also produce credible articles on the same questions for a news agency.

You have to choose one or the other!

Over and over again he came up against the same arguments, and I could see how it was getting him down.

It soon became clear that Stieg was working day and night. We used to say that he worked from 9.00 till 5.00 – 9.00 in the morning till 5.00 the next morning. There seemed to be no limit to what he needed to do: write articles; do research; coordinate editorial activities; buy coffee, loo rolls, bookcases, computers and toners for the printer . . . I didn't envy him, but I ought to have supported him more. My only consolation is that I know his pride would have prevented him from accepting more help than I gave him.

Every weekday at 1.30 he would turn up at the editorial office of either *Expo* or *Svartvitt*. He would bring a litre of milk for coffee, take a seat and talk before returning to his day job at T.T. He was back in the editorial office by 4.00. He told me that he often went to bed at about 5.00 in the morning. The last thing he always did was to switch off his mobile, which he both loved and hated.

We could see that he was pushing himself to the limit. His bloodshot eyes often betrayed his exhaustion. But I also remember the energy he radiated. Our collaboration was going well; we could look ahead with confidence and spent hours analysing the current state of democracy, or the latest move by some person or organization we both hated.

Then the day dawned when Stieg's book on Euro-Nat arrived from the printer's. Two weeks later we celebrated the publication of the first issue of the combined *Svartvitt* and *Expo* journals in my office. It was a memorable day. A lot of people called it a mad project. Perhaps they were right. But no matter; it was an act of madness that I shall never regret.

I remember clearly Stieg's pride when we sat in the editorial office with the new issue in our hands. How his voice boomed: "It's our obligation, damn it, to comment on and analyse and take the pulse of the new Sweden."

And then, when somebody produced a camera, how he displayed great agility in slipping off to one side and managing to avoid being in the picture. He was happy to take on work and share praise with others. But he made sure he didn't appear in any photographs if at all possible.

I sometimes wonder if Stieg had the same working habits

when he was younger. If he only had one gear: full steam ahead. Or whether the frenzy gathered pace later in his life. I would have loved to have seen him as an eighteen-year-old, doing his project on racism and political extremism. That assignment must have awakened something extraordinary in his frail teenage body. Perhaps that was a starting point for all that he came to stand for in adulthood as a journalist, author and lecturer.

"Kill your darlings," I used to tell Stieg when he was having trouble restricting himself. I often thought he was rather too fond of his own texts, and also those of others. It made no difference if it was a news article, a leaflet, a preface, a press release, a cultural article, a polemical essay or a chapter in a textbook.

I succeeded in becoming one of the very few people who were allowed to edit his texts ruthlessly. Not without him protesting loudly, of course. Quite early on, I hit upon a trick that seemed to work: cut half the text but allow the first four or five hundred words to stand unchanged, and find an appropriate way of summing up as the last sentence but one.

I don't suppose I shall ever see again anything like the driving force generated by Stieg when he was writing. I have never come across anybody who could write so easily and quickly the draft of a press release, a polemical article or a petition. And he seemed to be so happy as he did it. He could be hunched over and dog-tired, but when asked to write a press release, his whole body would straighten and his eyes light up.

Once as we were sitting in the Café Latte, he talked about his travels to Africa.

"Did you know I suffered from malaria while I was out there?"

"I had no idea."

He shrugged, and we spoke no more about it. But shortly afterwards we touched on the situation in Algeria.

"I once had a job there as a dishwasher. That was after a failed trip and I'd run out of money."

"You've done quite a lot of travelling."

"So have you," he said.

"That's true, that's one thing we have in common."

"'A woman's relationship to a man is like the slave's to the master, the manual labourer to the intellectual, the barbarian to the Hellene. A woman is an undeveloped man.'"

"Eh?"

"Who said that?"

"It must be some Greek philosopher," I said hesitantly, "in view of the word 'Hellene'."

"Aristotle."

How can one not miss conversations like that?

The period following our first joint issue was fantastic. Not least because we were proud of it, and of how well we had worked together. Then several things happened that shocked us deeply.

It started with the Malexander murders, one of the most discussed crimes of the 1990s in Sweden. In the course of a police chase following a bank robbery on 28 May 1999, two officers were shot dead with their own service revolvers. It seemed more like an out-and-out execution than anything else.

Only a few weeks later we received another horrific piece of news. Stieg and I were in the editorial office when the telephone rang on 28 June. A former member of the *Expo* staff, Peter Karlsson, his partner, Katarina Larsson, and their eight-year-old son had been victims of a car-bomb attack in the suburb of Nacka on 18 June. They had been rushed to hospital by helicopter, and we heard later that Peter had serious leg injuries. It came like a punch in the solar plexus to both Stieg and me. Threats were a normal part of our everyday life, but this was the nearest they had come to us personally.

Luckily Peter survived. What worried us most was that it ought not to have happened because Peter and his partner both carried alarm devices, but they hadn't gone off until a second before the explosion.

We could only interpret the assassination attempt on Peter and Katarina as a direct attack on *Expo*. Both of them had worked for the journal until quite recently. Their exposé in *Aftonbladet*, *Expressen* and *Dagens Nyheter* concerning so-called White Power music attracted a lot of attention, and seemingly was the reason for the outrage.

It was merely minutes after we'd heard the news ourselves that we began to receive a deluge of calls from the press. I sat with the receiver pressed to my ear; Stieg sat beside me writing a series of statements on Post-it notes. "Democracy cannot be taken for granted", "Every day and at every level of society we must fight for democracy, tolerance and respect". I read out what he had written, and could hear the reporters noting it down.

They asked how often we received death threats ourselves.

"All the time," I replied.

They wondered if it reminded me of my life in Kurdistan.

"That's an absurd comparison," I said as politely as I could.

Then a photographer arrived. He had been assigned to take pictures of the threats directed at *Svartvitt* and *Expo*. I produced an entire file full of threatening letters. He picked out examples that he considered to be "real threats" and was particularly interested in those decorated with swastikas.

Stieg, who had hidden himself away behind a computer screen, was grinning broadly and shaking his head. We both knew that news of this sort during the so-called silly season was a goldmine for hard-pressed editors. I would very much have liked to have passed them over to Stieg directly, but all I could do was get him to answer the telephone. He refused point blank to be photographed. As soon as he had a minute to spare, he wrote out new statements on our joint behalf. It was obvious how agitated he was.

"We can't just sit at home and allow the anti-democrats to take over the streets," he swore. He explained how far-right groups were associated especially with letter bombs. Moreover, he had heard that two neo-Nazis wanted by the police in Austria had gone to ground in Sweden and were being protected by people in Helsingborg linked with the far-right international organization Blood & Honour.

"There is a risk that they will take the opportunity to give Swedish neo-Nazis tips on how to make letter bombs," he said, lighting another cigarette.

Everybody in the editorial office was worried. How bad was the situation in reality? Was the attack on Peter an isolated event, or was it the first in a series? The mood was not improved when Stieg related in detail how a Danish neo-Nazi from the Blood & Honour network in Malmö had posted three letter bombs addressed to targets in England. We all knew that a Nazi sympathizer had been arrested the previous year at Stockholm-Arlanda Airport in possession of explosives.

Never before had we been in such complete agreement that we needed to mobilize as much opposition as possible.

"We must write a forceful manifesto. It's important that all well-known homosexuals, immigrants and women sign it," said Stieg, looking hard at me. "You can fix that. You know them."

"In that case I must have the final version as soon as possible so I can read it out to them. Damn it, it's the middle of summer – it won't be easy to get everything sorted at short notice."

That was all Stieg needed to hear. He raced over to my blue Apple Mac and seven minutes later he had finished our first joint petition.

All the celebrities we managed to get hold of signed it and on 7 July, 1999, the "Stop the Neo-Nazi and Racist Violence" petition was published in *Aftonbladet*:

> A neo-Nazi terrorist movement has grown up stealthily in Sweden. The worst fears seem to have been confirmed by the attempted assassination of the journalists Peter Karlsson and Katarina Larsson. Nevertheless, the recent car-bomb attack is only the tip of the iceberg. According to Säpo [the Swedish Security Service] 327 cases of assault on racist grounds took place in 1997.
>
> Peter Karlsson and Katarina Larsson are among the few who have blown the whistle on right-wing extremism in our society, which is becoming increasingly unsafe. And now, if not before, it is clear that it is not sufficient to talk about "drunken misbehaviour", "youthful folly" or "routine criminality", as we often hear from the police and authorities.

We, the signatories to this petition, therefore demand:

- That the security services finally acknowledge and prioritize the neo-Nazi terror and support the police in their work.
- That the police give adequate protection to people who are threatened by right-wing extremists.
- That the Minister of Justice draws up an action programme to get neo-Nazi and racist violence under control.
- That a crisis centre is established to assist the victims of racism.

Break the silence! We all have a responsibility to combat racism and neo-Nazism.

Everyone who wishes to live in a tolerant, democratic, humane and multicultural Sweden is urged to sign this petition . . .

Within twenty-four hours over a thousand signatures of ordinary Swedes were added to the petition. I asked Stieg to accompany me to Rosenbad, the prime minister's office, the following morning in order to hand over the list.

"A quarter to nine is too early for me. Besides, it would be better for a man and a woman born in different countries to go to the ministry."

I realized that it was a waste of time trying to persuade him and asked the journalist Bella Frank of the syndicalist newspaper *Arbetaren* to accompany me to hand the petition to Deputy Prime Minister Lena Hjelm-Wallén.

What none of us knew at the time was that it was already fifty-six days since a group of known neo-Nazis had ordered passport photographs and "current addresses" of Stieg, his partner, Eva, and me.

5

Living under threat

In the mid-1930s a terrifying and brutal gang of thugs ruled the roost in Syria. These five hundred dangerous men were led by the unpredictable Amo (Uncle). Every time they raided a restaurant they would instruct all the customers not to move. Then Amo would inspect all present and decide on punishments for them, each and every one. It was usually a question of how many gold coins each individual should pay. Anybody who refused was murdered on the spot.

The story goes that this notorious gang once forced its way into a nightclub in Aleppo that was very popular with well-heeled men in the early hours: they were all entranced by a beautiful belly dancer. But the moment Amo's gang entered the premises the four-man band stopped playing and everybody froze – including the belly dancer. To everyone's surprise Amo immediately ordered more music and more belly-dancing. The band struck up again and the belly dancer did her best to satisfy the customers.

When the performance had finished, Amo applauded and announced, "Today I shall only punish the musicians. The band will pay me one gold coin each – apart from the drummer, who will pay me three gold coins!" The poor drummer burst into tears and wondered why he had to pay more than the rest of the band. "You must pay more because I've noticed for a long time now that when the rest of the band is silent, the drums keep on disturbing the peace!"

Every time Stieg wondered why he was the one receiving death threats, I would tell him that story. It was an attempt to liven things up in a totally absurd situation. His vulnerability made him receptive to an anecdote that few Swedes would understand.

Stieg was the anti-racist musician who beat the drum whenever nobody spoke up concerning the principle that everybody had equal worth. Whenever silence fell – society so loves to sweep unpleasant phenomena under the carpet – he would be there, drumming away for all he was worth. The fact is that as early as the 1970s he had seen the danger of xenophobic, racist and neo-Nazi groups becoming organized in Sweden and the other Nordic countries. But nobody rewards you with bouquets of flowers for observations like that!

So his question about why he was being singled out for threats was purely rhetorical. Of course he knew the reason for the many long hate letters, and the way in which he was hung out to dry in racist magazines and on Internet sites. What is more difficult to explain, however, is why he replied to every single neo-Nazi, racist and xenophobic lunatic who sent him letters or issued threats. I simply could not understand why he spent hours replying to those people.

"If you don't reply to destructive people they will turn to destructive actions," he used to say, looking up from writing one such letter. Then he would carry on, also answering the next one even though it was late at night.

I don't know when and where these ghosts and phantoms first attacked Stieg, perhaps around the mid-1980s. It is hard to imagine any other Swede being threatened more often than he was during the last twenty years of his life. Nevertheless, he was very good at hiding his worries. Presumably so as not to worry anybody else, least of all Eva.

So what were his crimes, according to the racists? Obviously all the critical articles he wrote, his knack of seeing through their networks and activities. But his worst crime was probably that he was a blond-haired Swede who both supported and did his best to promote a "multicultural society". It was as if he had betrayed the racists.

The Swedish *National Encyclopedia* defines a traitor as "an individual who betrays a person or thing to which he or she is expected to be loyal". Perhaps that is how the racists regarded Stieg. Some countries only resort to the death penalty in cases of one kind: treason. Vidkun Quisling is in many ways the perfect example of how a person can betray his country. The way in which Stieg so doggedly opposed people and organizations who spoke about their country under the influence of their twisted view of humankind – well, it is easy to understand how he became a symbol for them. A symbol and a quarry to be hunted down.

I would even say that Stieg had a couple of bad habits. On the one hand, he was so considerate that he would often exaggerate threats aimed at people close to him. On the other hand, he would trivialize nearly all threats aimed at himself and did not take many precautions to protect himself from people who considered him to be dangerous.

He was shadowed by neo-Nazis whenever he travelled on the underground; racists kept an eye on him when he walked around Stockholm. They knew exactly where they had him. "I get off a stop before the one I'm actually going to," he would say diffidently. I sometimes felt like grabbing him by the shoulders and giving him a good shake. His unruffled behaviour, so typical of the north of Sweden, where he was born, could drive me up the wall. But he refused all suggestions – to keep changing his address (which I did at the time and still do), to accept free hotel passes (which I used to give him when things were especially threatening) or to go off on holiday when the situation became too tense (as I generally do when I don't feel safe in my flat).

"I get off a stop early."

In time our mutual enemies began to lump Stieg and me together. We had been in the business of fighting prejudice for a long time. We knew most of our tormentors. We were so experienced that we could tell from their handwriting if a person was dangerous or not. We regarded threats a bit like ordinary people examine the use-by date on a carton of milk. How current is this letter? This person has got tired by now, that's obvious. Ah, this one has struck a new note, don't you think?

We kept the whole business of threats at arm's length. Was that healthy? Probably not, but I think one's mind works like that so that one has the will to get up in the morning. In our darkest moments we both felt that we were living on borrowed time. Sooner or later something would happen.

Stieg was forty-five, I was thirty-four. We were grateful for the time we were being granted.

All the letter writers were men. Without exception. Young men and very old men.

The "November man" wrote threatening letters – but only in November. The "posh one" lived in Oskarshamn and wrote long, hate-filled rants, all in elegant Swedish. And then there was the "Thursday man", a tormentor approaching seventy who lived in Helsingborg. We had mixed feeling about him. We had first got to know him when he was fifty-eight and writing articles for a regional racist magazine. Should we feel sorry for him or take him seriously? What drives a person like that? We could never quite make him out. On the other hand, we were reluctantly impressed by his inexhaustible commitment, even if he was a bit short of ideas and kept repeating himself. Every week he collected articles that in one way or another dealt with the costs of immigration, and statistics on assaults committed in Sweden by people born abroad. In the margins he would make unpleasant notes, usually threatening murder, in red ink and with lots of exclamation marks.

It wasn't enough for him to send these threatening letters just to us. He would make a hundred photocopies of the ten most negative articles, put them in a hundred envelopes, and every Thursday, as punctually as a Swiss clock, address them to the hundred currently most active anti-racists. After twelve years it was clear that he was suffering more and more from dementia, but still he refused to stop writing these letters. Then one day he made a mistake. Instead of putting stamps on the hundred letters to anti-racists, he put ninety-nine stamps in an envelope that he posted to me, but forgot to stick stamps on the remaining ninety-nine letters. That meant that Stieg didn't receive a threatening letter from Helsingborg that week. We had a good laugh at the Thursday man's expense. And despite Stieg's protests I immediately put the stamps in our own postal kitty.

These tormentors have normal Swedish names, and often

seem to be drunk, especially when they telephone. Sometimes they have threatening voices; sometimes they sound like Donald Duck. The worst are those with deep voices who sound like cold-blooded murderers at the other end of the line. They always phone from public call boxes or from withheld numbers.

Both Stieg and I noticed that until January 1999, murder threats came almost exclusively after normal office closing time. Friday and Saturday evenings were especially popular. But then routines and methods started to change. The more serious callers threatening murder started to ring at about 9.00 in the morning. Presumably in order to disturb our working day more effectively.

Naturally there were a lot of others besides Stieg and me who were threatened – not least on the hate-filled racist websites. Their favourite targets were journalists, politicians, police officers, Holocaust survivors, immigrants, homosexuals, anti-racists, trade unionists and Swedes who had adopted non-white children.

As early as the beginning of the 1990s the neo-Nazis began to create their own secret police force. The force's remit was to identify anti-racist enemies and collect personal registration numbers, passport photographs and addresses of residences and workplaces. Thanks to the lax Swedish passport laws, these secret policemen had no difficulty in collecting passport photographs – all they had to do was to request passport information about the citizens in whom they were interested. There was not even any need to provide identification when they requested these sensitive details.

This negative aspect of the transparency principle led to several people losing their lives. On 12 October, 1999, the young trade unionist Björn Söderberg was murdered outside his flat in Sätra in southern Stockholm. This was the first time that a trade union activist had been murdered in Sweden. It is also a clear example of the price of standing up for one's beliefs. Söderberg was a syndicalist who refused to listen to racist music at his workplace and succeeded in getting a known neo-Nazi sacked. He would not accept the election of a neo-Nazi to the regional committee of the Commerce Employees' Association in Stockholm. This last stand was the equivalent of signing his own death warrant. Certain reports claimed that the Swedish police were keeping watch on the neo-Nazis patrolling outside his home.

Three days after Söderberg's murder, Stieg burst into *Svartvitt*'s office, gasping for breath. The first thing I noticed was that it was 9.00 in the morning. I soon realized why he was so upset. Unlike me, who receives his threatening letters in a post office box, Stieg had found his lying on the mat in his front hall.

"We have a lot to do," he said, sitting down. "First of all we need to look into how the police handled the build-up to the murder of Björn Söderberg. It's a scandal."

I made him a white coffee and watched him slump back in the light brown armchair, more or less exhausted.

"I don't understand," he said with a sigh, "why Söderberg received no practical advice from the police about how to go about your daily life when you've received murder threats. He ought to have known that he couldn't just open the door without first checking who had rung the bell."

"Nor was he allocated a police mentor after the neo-Nazis had got hold of his passport photograph."

"The worst thing of all," said Stieg, taking a swig of coffee, "is that the murder of Björn Söderberg could have been averted as easy as pie. The security police were shadowing the murderers as well as a third individual until half an hour before the murder."

Half an hour! We put that thought to the back of our minds. In other words, the security police were more or less on the spot when Björn Söderberg was shot dead.

Apart from being sad and upset about the murder, we had received a reminder of how dodgy our own situation was. It was obvious that we needed to do something. As usual, Stieg picked up his pen. After scribbling a few thoughts, he sat down at the computer.

A minute later, he had listed three points – or demands, as he called them.

- When the police discover a private individual on the hate list compiled by neo-Nazis, that person must be informed, no matter what.
- The police must be sensitive to the worry a threatened individual feels. He or she must be allocated a "mentor" from within the police.
- In extreme cases, the authorities must be willing to make a temporary safe house available to the people being threatened.

He handed me the printout to read. At the same time he opened his shoulder bag and produced a printout of an email.

"This came today," he said.

I read it.

Fuck fuck hooray! A nigger lover and traitor has been shot. We shall celebrate that this weekend, and demonstrate our support for our Aryan brothers who carried out this heroic deed. The armed campaign against those who betray their race and their country is only just beginning. Bullets have been reserved with your name on them. You will die, you nigger-loving swine.

I let the sheet of paper float down on to the desk.

"Why are you so agitated about this?" I wondered. "We get stuff like this all the time, and it's not even addressed to you personally."

But we both knew why we were feeling the pressure. It had become increasingly clear that 1999 was the year of demons. The situation had deteriorated appreciably in a very short space of time.

"It's about time we did something," Stieg said, leaning forward in the armchair. "We need to put this latest murder threat in the proper context. Two police officers have been killed by out-and-out racists. Two former colleagues have been car-bombed after investigating the racist music industry. A local councillor in Nybro has had his car blown up. The neo-Nazis have good contacts in the police force, which means that they often escape criminal proceedings. And now the syndicalist Björn Söderberg has been murdered in his own home."

"You reckon we should link all those happenings with this latest threat?"

"Exactly. Söderberg was murdered despite the fact that he had police protection. There are lots of people like us who have received murder threats. I've been investigating neo-Nazis for over twenty years, and I can say without hesitation that the situation today is more serious than it has ever been. There are those who think I'm a conspiracy theorist, but I think it's time to get to grips with the rotten eggs inside the Swedish police force."

He was furious. I had never seen him so agitated and irritated. The murder of Björn Söderberg had hit him hard. One explanation might be that Söderberg had been active in the same union as Stieg's mother, the Commerce Employees' Association. Söderberg's murder reminded Stieg of Vivianne, whom he had loved so much, so the cold-blooded execution became something personal.

"I think I get excellent help from the security police," I said, but he dismissed that statement with a wave of the hand.

"That's irrelevant. We must do something. Ring every journalist you know and tell them that the time has come when the government and the police must accept their responsibilities and act against racism. But just say that we and our colleagues are on the list, no more than that. I don't want to attract too much attention. We mustn't give the impression of being victims. It's a question of influencing public opinion. I think you should request an interview with the prime minister and ask that an anti-racist centre be established in Sweden."

I immediately joined the awkward squad.

"I'm fed up with telephoning journalists. But the idea of setting up a centre is good – very good."

"We need to get something in the newspapers."

"How about writing a polemical article and asking the editors of the biggest dailies – *Dagens Nyheter, Svenska Dagbladet,*

Expressen and *Aftonbladet* – to sign it and publish it the same day?"

"That sounds like a terrific idea."

"And as you have no intention of signing it," I said with a grin, "as a punishment you can write it."

He roared with laughter.

"Well, I'll be damned! Do you think they'll play along?"

"It's worth trying, don't you think?"

I saw him eyeing the new computer my secretary, Luciana, had bought the previous day.

"If you can get all the editors-in-chief on board," he said, rising to his feet, "I'll provide you with the best text I've ever written."

The very next minute I heard him tapping away at the keyboard as if his life depended on it.

Even if Stieg was always most upset when somebody else had been threatened, there is no getting away from the fact that he himself was more vulnerable than anyone. The worst thing from his point of view was not how he was affected, but what effect his being affected had on his partner, Eva. When we heard that a woman with clear neo-Nazi links and her 23-year-old son had collected passport photographs of him, Eva and me, the situation became even more serious. The same people had acquired passport photographs of Peter and his partner, Katarina, before they had been car-bombed.

We realized that we needed to take measures to increase our security. The problem for Stieg was that he had an ambivalent relationship with the police, which was not difficult to understand. He was forced to ask them for help, but at the same time he was always criticizing the way they carried out their duties.

In all the conversations we had about the threats we received, he stressed that it was Eva he was concerned about. She was his lifeline, and he insisted that he would never forgive himself if she was affected by something that could be traced back to his anti-racist activities.

I often suggested that they should go away for a holiday when things became too strained, but every time he just shook his head.

I have a particular memory of our countless discussions about the threats we faced. We had been talking for an unusually long time and eventually came round to the same old conclusion: I had proposed that we should lie low for a while, and suggested yet again that he and Eva should go away for a week or two. This time he actually said that he would talk to her about the situation. He didn't fancy it himself, but perhaps it would be good for her to get away.

When we said goodbye on the stone steps down to the front door, Stieg turned to me and said, "If only you knew the danger you and I are in."

That was all. We nodded to each other and he vanished into the dark street.

Two days later Stieg was guilty of professional misconduct at T.T. He wrote about the neo-Nazi threats aimed at himself and three colleagues at *Expo*.

Obviously, Stieg knew all the rules governing news journalism like the back of his hand. Even so, his text lacked the neutrality, impartiality and relevance required of a professional journalist. He actually went so far as to interview his own editor at *Expo*.

He was aware, of course, that it was wrong of him to write about threats aimed at himself and his colleagues.

I was extremely upset. Obviously I knew the pressure he was under – he had just resigned from T.T., and would soon receive two years' salary. Moreover, nobody else had noticed his violation of the rules. But that is what it was and I thought it unworthy of him.

I wept over my friend's error.

6

The infiltrator

Parties and party leaders can and should disagree about most factual matters in this world of ours. This is one of the rules of the game where democracy is concerned. Politics develops from these conflicting views.

But there are exceptions. There are some questions fundamental to our communal values where there can and must be no differences of opinion in a democratic society.

Among them is the struggle against racism, anti-Semitism and intolerance of minorities.

Anti-democratic and extreme movements that call into question our open society and the equal status of all human beings must be opposed by all means at our disposal. This is a battle we must fight together.

We party leaders represent different views and different values, which in combination represent an absolute majority of the Swedish people. We are all agreed on this. All people are of equal value, irrespective of skin colour, language, gender, religion, ethnic background or sexual orientation. This is the foundation on which the humanitarian and democratic principles of our society are based.

In the last analysis, we all have a moral responsibility to stand up and be counted in support of these values whenever and wherever they are called into question – to fight against injustice, to protect the rights of the

individual and to make a contribution to mutual understanding between all people.

Tomorrow is 30 November – a date that has become
something of an unofficial rallying day for Swedish
racism. That is why we say today: We shall never submit
to intolerance!

*Göran Persson (Prime Minister, Social Democrats), Bo
Lundgren (leader, Conservatives), Lars Leijonborg (leader,
Liberals), Alf Svensson (leader, Christian Democrats),
Lennart Daléus (leader, Centre Party), Gudrun Schyman
(leader, Left Communists), Lotta Hedström (spokeswoman,
Green Party), Kurdo Baksi (editor-in-chief,* Svartvitt *with*
Expo*)*

The "We shall never submit" appeal, published on 29 November,
2000, is probably the text Stieg Larsson was proudest of having
written. When I first read it in the bar of the Amaranten Hotel,
that much was obvious in my friend's face. Although his name is
not mentioned, he was responsible for every single word. My
only contribution was to lobby various people with close links to
the party leaders.

Stieg gave me a big hug when we met at the Amaranten. This
was an unusually intimate gesture, occasioned by the fact that I
had kept the promise I had made to him: to make sure that
an appeal from all Swedish political party leaders would be
published on that particular day in November by four national
daily newspapers based in Stockholm, plus thirty or so regional
newspapers.

The fact is that it was quite easy to convince the party leaders to sign, even if I think I spared Stieg the fact that the one who was hardest to get on board was the prime minister, Göran Persson. This surprised me, because Persson was the one with whom I had the best contacts. In the end it was thanks to Jenny Ohlsson, one of Persson's assistants, that I managed to retain Stieg's words more or less intact.

It was obvious how much this meant to Stieg. This was one of the most important moments in our friendship. Not just because of the success we had with the appeal, but also because it was the day we had one of our most heated quarrels.

The Amaranten bar was more or less empty, as usual. It suited us to meet there – it was quiet and relaxed, with luxurious if slightly grubby decor. Looking back, it is easy to conclude that a friendship without frank discussions is doomed in advance. Such a friendship can never progress beyond the polite and the conventional.

When we sat down in the bar, I had been angry with Stieg for quite some time. Perhaps it was our recent successes that gave me the courage to raise the matter. Ever since I had heard that one of the younger members of *Expo*'s staff had infiltrated some of the parties linked with neo-Nazism using a false name, I had been nagged by worry. Obviously I was concerned about the young man's safety. But I was just as concerned that the media would attack *Expo* again. The journal would not be able to survive another collapse in subscriber numbers.

It had taken two years for *Expo* to repair the damage caused the previous time it had lost its journalistic self-respect.

I knew I had to ask Stieg the question, it simply had to be done.

"Stieg," I said, after taking a swig of beer, "where do you think the boundary is between a journalist using false names and identities in order to obtain information, and infiltrating an organization?"

It seemed as if he had been expecting the question. He responded without hesitation.

"If a neo-Nazi party, or a party linked with neo-Nazism, refuses to provide information about its activities and refuses to answer questions, it is legitimate to obtain information in unconventional ways."

I didn't reply, but sat in silence for a while. It was obvious that Stieg was irritated. He almost spat out, "Normal journalistic techniques get nowhere with neo-Nazi groups. So what do you expect us to do? Sit back with our arms folded?"

Sighing, I realized that the discussion had already become more heated than I had hoped it would.

"I understand what you mean, but I don't agree. There are limits, even in investigative journalism. How and when you should resort to false identities requires a long discussion. There are various ways for a journalist to pretend to be somebody else in order to find out information that is difficult to get hold of."

He leaned back in his chair, as if waiting to hear what I would say next. It was not at all like him to allow me to speak without interruption, but perhaps it was obvious that I really was worried and angry.

"The question is," I went on, "how one should react when undercover journalism becomes a matter of life and death. Placing a young person in a neo-Nazi or racist organization is a big responsibility. There is a constant risk that somebody might be injured or even murdered. Surely you can see the danger with this business of using a false identity? It could end in tragedy."

I felt almost breathless after speaking so fast. It was clear that Stieg was annoyed. He shook his head.

"We have a member of staff who volunteered to do this. I would never force anybody to undertake such a dangerous assignment in order to uncover information. But what I do do is give our colleague maximum support."

"How?"

"By protecting and being in constant touch with him. We have set up clear rules for how he should go about things. He must not spread racist propaganda, nor is he allowed to take initiatives leading to neo-Nazi campaigns. In addition we have another colleague close to where he is located."

Now it was my turn to shake my head. I was not at all satisfied with his answer. This was a kind of life-and-death game that I couldn't possibly accept.

"*Expo* has always received tips from rival neo-Nazi groups. And a lot of their members resign when they get reach thirty and start families. We are journalists, Stieg, not bloody police officers!"

Stieg reacted in a way I'd never seen him react before. He glanced quickly round the bar, which was just as deserted as it had been earlier. Then he looked me straight in the eye and raised his voice. It was both angry and reproving in a way I wasn't at all happy about.

"The police!" he said, raising a finger. "What did they do when *Expo*'s printer was attacked? What did they do when the neo-Nazis shot at your flat? What did they do when Peter was car-bombed? Why did their surveillance arrangements fall short when a trade unionist was murdered? Why did it take them four months to tell us that somebody had collected our passport photos? Were they waiting for us to be murdered as well?"

"I think you're exaggerating."

"My point is that the police don't take racism and neo-Nazism seriously. It's not exactly news to you that there are neo-Nazis in the Swedish police force, is it?"

"No."

"So why are you defending the police? Surely you haven't forgotten that neo-Nazi millionaire in Filipstad who controlled a considerable network within the Swedish police? When three Latin Americans were beaten up in Gamla Stan in Stockholm, one of the neo-Nazis arrested turned out to be the son of that multi-millionaire. Was he ever put in a police cell? Was he ever charged?"

Stieg was now so het up that there was no point in trying to calm him down. It was as if several years of frustration were gushing forth as he sat in the bar. I began to accept that I was doomed to be the day's target. My problem was that I agreed with his analysis, but in no circumstances could I support him in what he considered to be the most effective way of dealing with the situation.

I let him continue with his lecture, but could not support his plans to infiltrate the neo-Nazis.

Eventually he leaned back in the armchair again and took a swig of beer. He was still annoyed, but now he said in a calmer voice, "You must get more up to date with what's going on, Kurdo. Nowadays neo-Nazis can be between ten and eighteen years old. A lot of them start a family, get a steady job, carry a briefcase, wear a suit and tie, and still continue to be active neo-Nazis. Do you know that several high-ranking police officers maintain that you yourself organized the shooting at your flat?"

Hmmm, the shooting at my flat in Tensta, just outside Stockholm. What happened during the night of 3 November, 1999? A horrific incident that is practically impossible to explain to somebody who wasn't there. Half the living room was covered in shards of glass. I was attacked despite the fact that I was being protected by neighbours and the police. I had often asked myself how one could avoid being subjected to neo-Nazi violence. I had several offices in different locations, several flats so that I could move from one to the other, unarmed bodyguards, special protection on public occasions, frequent conversations with the police about safety measures, contact with a police mentor, irregular working hours, taxi rides, taking different routes to and from my offices and flats. Even so, one never feels safe.

I had only myself to blame for our conversation taking the course it did. I was the one who had initiated the discussion. Nevertheless, I couldn't simply let pass what I had just heard. How could my friend allow somebody to risk his life by infiltrating the neo-Nazis, who had so much blood on their hands? The shooting at my flat wasn't even one of their worst crimes.

All I knew at that stage was that one of *Expo*'s reporters had spent two years, 1997–9, embedded in the inner circle of a neo-Nazi-inclined group in Blekinge. In a roundabout way I had heard that it was in accordance with Stieg's wishes that this person had become a member of the extremist group, which was steeped in criminal activity.

I had suspected this for some time before discovering that it was in fact the case. Nevertheless, I had done nothing about it until that evening. The reason I had lain low for so long was that *Expo* and *Svartvitt* had two separate editorial boards. That was the arrangement we had agreed upon from the start, and I couldn't simply barge in and comment on *Expo*'s editorial policies.

But now I had realized that our friendship would not be able to survive this clash of ideas. It was dependent on our being able to resolve differences of opinion like this. Moreover, to be completely honest, I wasn't absolutely certain that I was right. I simply didn't know if our two boards would be able to continue cooperating. I didn't even know if the relationship between Stieg and me would survive the strain.

"Stieg," I said with a sigh, "we are talking about a seventeen-year-old. How can you possibly think that it's acceptable for such a young person to infiltrate such a dangerous group? Still, nothing awful has happened, so we can draw a line under it. We must look to the future. You must promise me one thing: in no circumstances will you allow anybody under the age of eighteen to do anything as dangerous as this again. Neo-Nazis know no limits. They are capable of anything. We don't have the right to expose anyone else to danger, irrespective of how important the information is that *Expo* is trying to track down. You always say that the right to life takes precedence over everything else. That must apply to *Expo*'s staff as well."

Stieg said nothing. He stared at me for quite a while, rubbing his knees. Then he looked as if he had had second thoughts. He folded his hands over his stomach and sighed. He lit a cigarette and offered me one. We both inhaled.

"You are right," he said.

We sat there in silence, smoking. It was impossible to know what he was thinking. Suddenly he said, "You must have lunch with Erland the next time you give a lecture in Umeå."

"Who's that?"

"My dad."

"Stieg, you mustn't call your father Erland, that's rude. You should simply say 'my dad'."

We both laughed. We weren't quite sure why we laughed, I suspect. Perhaps because the difference between his background in the north of Sweden and mine in Turkish Kurdistan had suddenly become so obvious.

"I promise," I said with a smile, "to have lunch with your father the next time I'm in Umeå. It will be an honour."

Then we struggled up out of our comfortable hotel armchairs. Stieg collected his rucksack and we went out into the chill of Kungsholmsgatan. We shook hands as colleagues and best friends. Our friendship had passed the test. It was as if we breathed a mutual sigh of relief.

A year later I heard that Stieg had been one of the instigators behind another member of the *Expo* staff – a mere twenty years old – becoming an infiltrator into a neo-Nazi-inclined xeno-phobic group.

7

The sleepless warrior

It is impossible to describe Stieg without mentioning his insomnia. The man seemed never to sleep. He was aware of this and we often spoke about it. One conclusion we came to was that there are people who manage to do their jobs efficiently despite sleeping very little at night. When it comes to comparing him with insomniacs like Churchill and Napoleon, however, I sometimes have the feeling that Stieg had something else in common with them: he was always ready to do battle. The difference being that the battles Stieg fought always took place in the mind, in mental arenas. I would call them battles over human values.

I occasionally used to say that Stieg was a sleep saver. Maybe there is no such expression, but I always thought it suited him. He admitted that even as a child he had found it difficult to go to bed in the evening. He had become a night owl early on, despite the fact that his constant curiosity and his eagerness to work meant that he was driven to be just as active during the day.

We often discussed whether sleeping well resulted in a longer life. Looking back, it feels uncomfortable to recall those many discussions; we agreed it did not necessarily follow that people who always slept well accomplished more. We could think of too many cases where the opposite applied.

One might even ask if it is possible for any dedicated and committed person, always involved in hundreds of projects, to sleep well. How can a good-hearted individual relax when human rights are being violated on a daily basis? When there are people with no roofs over their heads? When there are millions of refugees in the world? For somebody unacquainted with Stieg, such questions might sound somewhat naive and illogical; but in all our conversations these undeniable facts were an overwhelming driving force that empowered his will to change things.

The fact is that Stieg himself sometimes compared his sleeping habits to Churchill's. He used to say that they were in the same league when it came to insomnia, but that the old statesman had the edge. Apparently Churchill seldom slept for more than three hours per night. Nevertheless he lived to the ripe old age of ninety, as Stieg never failed to point out when I or somebody else complained about his bad nocturnal habits.

I suggested that the number of hours one slept was not the most important thing. When you sleep is also crucial. Stieg usually went to bed when most other people were getting up. I don't actually know if the time when you sleep is all that significant in fact, I suppose I just wanted to see him properly rested – something as unlikely to happen as our bringing about peace. Tired, red eyes, irregular breathing and slowing reflexes spoke for themselves. Winning the peace, as we used to put it, was the greatest achievement possible.

If Churchill had his champagne and cigars, Stieg had his coffee and cigarettes. Not such a grand combination, one has to admit. I know nobody who was as inveterate a smoker as Stieg. He had been chain-smoking since he was a teenager and it was hard to imagine him not puffing away at a cigarette. Coffee was his second greatest love. Churchill wanted his champagne "cold, dry and free", and Stieg wanted his coffee with milk but no sugar.

Most of all, he wanted lots of it. There was no limit to the amount of coffee he could drink. I have never come across anybody as hooked on caffeine as Stieg. When we spent sixteen hours together at Prime Minister Persson's international conference on the Holocaust, I kept a count of how many servings of coffee Stieg drank. I made it twenty-two, most of them plastic mugs.

That amount of coffee can hardly be conducive to decent sleep. Swilling down twenty or so cups of coffee a day and smoking two or three packets of cigarettes no doubt ruin more than just a decent night's slumber. They must slowly but surely undermine your whole body.

The slim, elegant young man I had met at the Vasa restaurant in the autumn of 1992 started to acquire chubby cheeks. His body became increasingly bloated, and he needed to buy bigger trousers and shirts. He had no interest at all in food. He ate if and when he had the time. Usually greasy junk food. But his weight increase had no effect on his energy, his enthusiasm for work or his lust for life. He was always smiling. It is true to say that he became more and more stressed as the years went by, but he never lost focus or became distrait.

He would spend most of his time glued to his computer, focusing all his attention first on one project, then on the next. Full speed ahead all the time. Interestingly enough, he was always motionless in front of his screen. The only part of his body he kept in trim was his brain – the rest of him had to survive as best it could.

I frequently suggested that he take up swimming. He thought that sounded even worse than going for walks in the woods. He would often grasp at any excuse to avoid having to listen to all the nagging – he was under constant threat of being murdered, he couldn't possibly risk anything of the sort. That would be reckless in the extreme. He had a point, of course: but his main reason was to avoid taking any physical exercise. He very rarely did anything of the sort. He never stopped smoking, although he did cut down during the last year or so of his life. I occasionally saw him taking snuff as well.

Whenever he thought I was nagging him too much, Stieg would tell me that he was about to take his annual fortnight's holiday. When I asked if he was going to leave his computer at home, he would always change the subject.

You can imagine how astonished I was to hear that in his younger days, he took part in skiing competitions. That sounds so unlikely. I have never been able to establish how good he was, but the very fact that he must once have been sufficiently interested to enter flabbergasts me. I have never met anybody less interested in sport – never ever.

My friend Stieg Larsson was one of those people who believe in their own immortality. He was in good company. Most people think that accidents only happen to others. But I know that he sometimes thought about how his mother had died far too early from a cerebral haemorrhage. This was a great sorrow always at the back of his mind. She died at the age of fifty-six in Erland's arms, one summer's day in 1991, as he was combing her hair. Shortly before her death she had read Stieg's newly published book on the Extreme Right, *Extremhögern*, at a single sitting.

No, there is no explanation for the way in which Stieg waged war on his own body. Nor would he ever be able to explain it himself. More than anything else it was like a vicious circle that could not be broken.

Yet again I come back to the contradictory nature of Stieg's character. That overwhelming work ethic – most probably made even stronger by his working-class background – which he insisted on forcing others to adopt. And then the direct opposite: a total inability to discipline himself when it came to looking after his own body. Worst was, of course, his lack of sleep, and perhaps his complete lack of discipline in this respect was due to what the medics call insomnia. Anybody suffering from this complaint can seldom get to sleep for any reason other than utter exhaustion.

For Stieg it was a case of working until 5.00 or 6.00 in the morning, then falling asleep worn out. Only a few hours later he would start a new day by taking breakfast and reading a book and newspapers in a café. Then he would go first to the *Svartvitt* editorial office, then to *Expo* and embark on another packed working day.

The doctors I have spoken to point out that insomnia can be dangerous, especially if it persists for a long time. In Stieg's case it probably lasted for the whole of his working life. They say it can be hereditary, but I have found nothing in Stieg's past to suggest that this applies to his case. I asked Erland, his father, about it.

"No," he said, "I sleep soundly at night and nobody else in the family has ever had any trouble getting to sleep."

I met Erland on 19 March, 2001. It was in Umeå and the whole town was covered in snow. Later that evening I was due to give a lecture in Mimerskolan about the integration of youngsters with an immigrant background into Swedish society.

Quite a long time had passed since Stieg and I had begun to call each other big brother and kid brother. They had become our nicknames, even though we only used them when we were alone together. That was also how I had introduced myself to Erland when I'd phoned to arrange our meeting. "Stieg said that as I am his kid brother, I must have lunch with Dad." Erland had had a good laugh at our absurd way of addressing each other.

The first thing that struck me when I met Erland was how amazingly young he looked. So it was not difficult to work out where Stieg had got that trait from. Erland was wearing a dark cardigan and a black shirt. It was easy to infer that he came from northern Sweden, not just because of his dialect but also because of a tendency to express himself in few words without unnecessary embellishment. His eyes also seemed to wander as he talked, something I took to be linked to the Norrland shyness of which I had become so fond.

The moment we finished our salad, Erland said, "Stieg ought to visit me more often. What's he up to in Stockholm? He always sounds so stressed. It would be good if the three of us could meet some time."

I immediately tried to explain what kept Stieg so busy. It was a long explanation, but Erland listened intently as we sat at our window table. What I really wanted to get across was how Stieg's work was the very breath of life for him; it wasn't a question of stress in the usual sense of the word. When Erland and I said our goodbyes, we decided that we would definitely arrange that lunch with Stieg. "Then it will be my turn to get the bill," I insisted.

Stieg, Erland and I never did manage to have lunch together. The fact is that we only once met, the three of us, and that was in a Stockholm hospital. In order to write about that moment, so painful and inscribed for ever in my memory, I have needed to gather my strength for four and a half years. That was how long it took before I was able to start writing this book.

As I sit thinking about this, I find myself returning again and again to one particular thing. I think about Stieg and his fight to ensure that one day he would win the peace. When that day came, we used to say, he would finally be able to get a good night's sleep.

8

The feminist compromise

For four years in succession, on International Women's Day – 8 March – I have handed out a thousand roses to women in Sergels Torg in Stockholm. I have frequently felt a bit ambivalent about this celebration, initiated in 1910 by the German Communist and champion of women's rights Clara Zetkin. I think it would be preferable for every day to be imbued with a recognition of gender rights rather than just one day per year.

Then again, it is good to have a day on which to honour the millions of women who have been victims of male supremacy for thousands of years. For me personally, it is also a day to pay homage to my friend Stieg Larsson. So my thousand roses also direct my thoughts to him. He was always impressed by effective symbolic actions.

Most of the women to whom I present a rose are pleased. I am hugged by a lot of young and elderly ones. It warms the heart. But naturally, not everybody is pleased. Quite a few young women tell me, "Yes to equality, no to a rose." In a way, I understand them. I even feel a bit embarrassed. Perhaps I ought not to continue doing this next year. After all, roses have thorns.

I am quite sure that Stieg and I hit upon this idea together. But then, maybe we should also have considered handing out roses to men, in an attempt to persuade them to behave better. To encourage them. Perhaps the thorns would have been more appropriate when roses were offered to men.

It doesn't really matter. Like everything else, the distribution of roses has something egotistical about it. I enjoy buying them and distributing them. It turns my thoughts to the conversations Stieg and I used to have about everything under the sun. The oppression of women was something we often discussed, not least because it was a subject on which he was an expert. I don't think there are many people who know more about how things came to be like that, and what horrific consequences this could have.

In the course of a few months at the end of 2001 and the beginning of 2002, two incidents took place that affected Stieg personally and emotionally, and were of great significance for his work. I am referring to the murders of Melissa Nordell in November 2001 in Stockholm and of Fadime Sahindal in January 2002 in Uppsala. The young photographer's model Melissa Nordell was murdered by her Swedish boyfriend, who was older than she was, simply because he refused to respect her wish to break off their relationship. Every time Melissa's name or fate was mentioned, Stieg's eyes would fill with tears. There was no way he could accept that a young Swedish woman could be denied her freedom simply because she was a woman. He scrutinized all the accessible legal documents and newspaper articles about Melissa Nordell, and also contacted her family. Stieg even became a friend of Melissa's mother and her stepfather, and invited them to a party for our employees in my office. I shall never forget my meeting with Melissa's mother. It is an irony of fate that the last book cover Stieg was responsible for included a colour photograph of Melissa Nordell.

Alongside the picture of Melissa on that same cover was one of the young Swedish-Kurdish woman Fadime Sahindal, who was murdered by her father one cold January night in 2002. Fadime died for one reason alone: she wanted to lead her own life, go her own way. The murder of Fadime shook Stieg on many levels – personally, ideologically and as a journalist – and raised several questions: should he analyse it exclusively from the point of view of gender, or should he also take account of her ethnicity, genetic make-up, religion and culture? Stieg repeatedly told me that in his view it was the patriarchal regime that cost the lives of these young women. When I suggested that he should explain his point of view in articles for the daily newspapers, he told me that he would prefer to "write a book about the oppression of women in order to make my position clear". In January 2004 he published the anthology *Debatten om hedersmord* (The Honour Killings Debate) under the *Svartvitt* imprint.

I recall a conversation Stieg and I had in January 2002. The horrific events had sparked off one of the most important debates in recent Swedish history: about honour killings and vulnerable girls in patriarchal cultures. The tone of the debate became more and more confrontational, and created two camps fighting each other on television chat shows, in radio debates and in articles in the biggest newspapers. Anti-racists were attacked for encouraging honour killings and feminists were accused of encouraging racism.

Stieg would sometimes amuse himself by presenting us with various quotations, challenging us to identify the sources. For him it was all a sort of game.

"'Nature,'" he would say, looking mischievous, "'has landed

women with broad hips and a large bottom – and hence has obviously indicated that women should sit around and look after the house.'"

"No idea. Maybe some mullah or other in Iran?"

"Wrong. Martin Luther."

It was obvious how pleased he was when our guesses were so wide of the mark. It was as if that proved the thesis he was putting forward.

"How about this one, then? 'The fundamental fault of the female character is that it has no sense of justice.'"

"Arthur Schopenhauer."

To my great surprise I was sometimes able to guess correctly. That would earn me a nod of acknowledgement.

But on this occasion, I couldn't resist turning the heat up a bit. I said, "You like to quote white European men. But surely you're not suggesting that women outside Europe have a better time of it than European women? According to Muslim sharia law, a woman may inherit only half of what a man can inherit. The evidence of two women is the equivalent of that of one man, and in many parts of the world women are not allowed to choose their own partners, or have control of their own bodies. There must be different levels in hell, surely?"

I had the impression that Stieg's thoughts had shot off somewhere else. He liked to be opposed, but at the same time disliked it. Stieg the snorting warhorse had been aroused. The quotation game was fun, but this was something completely different. This inspired his fighting spirit. He enjoyed arguments and liked to be provoked, provided it was at the right level and on the right day.

"O.K.," he said, "what conclusions can we draw? Women are

oppressed globally. Every day, all over the world, women are mutilated, murdered, ill-treated, circumcised, by men rich and poor. It might happen in South Africa, Saudi Arabia, Norway, Mexico, Tibet or Iran. But the fact is that there's no such thing as soft or hard oppression of women: men want to own women, they want to control women, they are afraid of women. Men hate women. The oppression of women has nothing to do with religion or ethnicity."

He was obviously agitated. It was as if he had listened to his own words and was furious about the way things were in the world. That very day I had also been attacked in several polemical articles on honour killings. *Expressen*'s leader page was particularly scathing about me. Obviously, Stieg was aware of this. He had read every word, and I knew that he wished me well. But now he had gone into his characteristic fighting mode, and had no intention of mincing his words in order to spare me.

At first I thought he was just a bit annoyed with me, but I soon realized that in fact he was really upset and disappointed.

"I get so angry with you," he said, staring hard at me. "Just like all the rest of the polemicists, you never mention both Fadime's first and family names when you write about her. That's unacceptable. You can't afford not to give a murdered woman's full name. *You* especially can't afford that."

"You never get the questions you want to answer in an interview or a debate," I said. "You have to answer the questions the media put to you."

He didn't want to listen to excuses like that, and brushed the argument aside with a snort.

"The relative status of the sexes is all too obvious in what journalists write about criminal cases. Male victims are always given their full names in the newspapers. How names are used is related to a person's position and status in society. That's what I want you to understand. You must always use Fadime's first and family names in future."

I promised to do so, but he was far from finished with me. He had got into his stride and I could tell that he was about to launch into a lecture. It was impossible to stop him.

"I'll tell you why this debate is being buggered up," he said, gesticulating wildly.

"Please do."

"Some of the people taking part are adherents of a traditional pattern of explanation. According to them, Fadime Sahindal was killed for sexist reasons. In other words, her murderer's ethnicity and religion are completely irrelevant."

He leaned forward and continued.

"Then there are those who are completely wrong. Those are the ones who look for explanations in cultural anthropology. In their eyes Fadime Sahindal was killed because her murderer is a Kurd who grew up in a Muslim environment. They are defenders of ethnocentric cultural relativism. According to them there are *different kinds* of oppression of women. The cultural anthropological explanation only informs us about the form the oppression takes, not about the cause. Assaults on women on Saturday nights in Sweden, honour killings in Italy, the burning of women in India and the stoning of women in Iran in fact tell us the same thing: men in patriarchal societies oppress women."

"What about the media?" I asked. "They want to devote themselves to comparative studies of female oppression. Which continent is the worst for women? In which culture or religion do women have the most freedom? The media try to simplify answers to provide headlines. Complicated explanations or answers don't sell copies, do they?"

Stieg was able to go along with the suggestion that everybody, not least the pair of us, was trapped by the media's constant search for striking headlines and simplified explanations. Nevertheless he dismissed that argument and continued his lecture, more het up than ever.

"The problem is that all this results in our falling into the right-wing extremists' trap. As if ethnicity and cultural background decide a human being's value. They thrive on racist concepts and national stereotypes. Racists maintain that European culture is superior to all others. That's why they always talk about 'us' and 'them'. According to them, immigrants don't have an enlightened view of women, but Swedes do."

It had become pitch black outside the window of our basement room. Another ice-cold January day was drawing to a close. I think we both knew that basically we were in agreement. But there was something in the situation that made Stieg want to continue plugging away at his argument. The only difference between hundreds of other discussions and this one was that his irritation was now directed at me.

"The fact is that only men oppress women," he said. "Everything else is a lot of crap. You are letting the cultural chauvinists railroad the debate. The consequence will be that the Sweden Democrats will get even more votes and win more seats on the local councils. The debate about the murder of Fadime Sahindal can have terrible consequences. Feminism and anti-racism go together. That's what you must make people understand. On no account must you accept that there is a special kind of oppression of women peculiar to Kurds. When immigrant men kill, they say it's due to their foreign culture and failed integration policies. When Swedish men kill it's because they've been drinking too much strong booze."

"You're right there," I said. "If we were to follow the cultural anthropological argument we could just as well say that the murder of the police officer in Malexander was caused by the inherent evil of Swedish Christianity."

"Exactly. Do you know what the best thing you've said in this debate is?"

"I didn't realize that I'd said anything reasonable at all," I said with a wry smile.

"It was when you said that Kurds didn't have a monopoly on the oppression of women. That is correct, and illuminating. And I realize that you will have some trouble with Kurdish exile groups in Sweden. They are bound to ask you to tone down the debate on the oppression of women and honour killings."

I nodded. He was absolutely right; I knew I was going to get into hot water. Even worse than usual.

Perhaps he noticed that, because he said, "I don't envy you. Immigrants, Swedes and Kurds will all question your loyalty. They will force you to take sides. In order to regard themselves as good, some people pick out others and call them bad. You must keep a cool head and not fall into the cultural trap. We need to win this debate."

"I don't know if we *can* win this debate."

He was on the point of saying something, but for once it was me who interrupted him.

"More and more Kurdish girls feel that it's the Kurdish or Muslim culture that is behind horrific incidents such as honour killings. That's not entirely irrelevant."

I got up to fetch the latest edition of *Expressen*. Without our noticing, the whole office had become completely dark. Outside the window was a solitary street lamp. I felt I had been attacked by my friend. Obviously I knew that he wanted to help me. He wanted to warn, protect and support me. He was doing that as best he could. I ought to have been grateful, but I could feel that my irritation had increased thanks to his vitriolic sermon.

When I switched on the lamp it suddenly struck me how remarkably light and darkness interact. Before, we had been hidden, but now the only darkness was outside the window. At a stroke anybody could see what was going on inside the office. I had that familiar feeling of vulnerability. How can you explain to somebody who has never experienced it what it's like, always to be living alongside a powerful but nevertheless indefinable enemy? Somebody who can see you the moment you switch on the light and who follows every step you take. Luckily, most people never have to think about things like that.

I even surprised myself when I slammed the newspaper down on the table. The article's headline was staring at us: "Choose sides – now!"

"Don't you understand, Stieg," I said, "that the Kurds' spokesmen are worried about being blamed for the murder of Fadime Sahindal? But it's not the media attention that's the problem. The problem is the organizations that represent groups from the

Middle East and North Africa. Kurdish women need the media attention they are getting. Believe me, I am a man who was born in Kurdistan. It's not so bloody easy for me to represent Kurdish women."

"I understand that, Kurdo, I understand that."

"Most of those contributing to the debate think that honour killings are arranged by the victim's family. In other words, that the phenomenon is socially acceptable. But if I understand you rightly, you're saying that murderers who kill women in the Western world are individuals who make their own decisions and act individually. Am I right?"

"No, you're not. Take 22-year-old Melissa Nordell. She was Swedish and dumped her considerably older boyfriend. He refused to let her go, and in the end attacked her. He raped her and tortured her with a stun gun. Then, to top it all off, he throttled her. When he realized what he had done, he phoned a relative who was a company director or something of the sort. Between them they cleaned up the scene of the murder, wrapped the corpse in chicken wire and dumped it on the island of Ingarö. Do you remember that?"

"Of course I do."

"The boyfriend was jailed for life and his relative got two years for desecration of a grave. The newspapers called it a *crime passionnel*."

"I take your point, Stieg. I understand that the difference between these two murders is purely cosmetic. You don't need to be Einstein to get that. It's just that there's nobody in this country who wants to listen to such arguments right now. Fadime Sahindal's father murdered her because he couldn't accept the fact that she insisted on going her own way. Melissa Nordell was murdered by her ex-boyfriend because he couldn't accept the fact that she was going to leave him. Neither woman was allowed to go her own way. That's why they were punished."

"That's how we must express ourselves in the media. Exactly like that."

For the first time in our conversation Stieg looked pleased. It was as if we both heaved a sigh of mutual relief. Neither of us had looked at the clock yet. It felt as if night had fallen.

Then Stieg leaned towards me and said, in a voice much more intimate than before, "I'm prepared to do anything at all to get this debate about honour killing on the right track."

"Then you can start by writing a really good polemical article," I said.

"O.K. But not in my name. I can't represent the Kurdish point of view. I was born in Skelleftehamn, you were born in Kurdistan. I can support you. Once the debate is over – and that could take more than a year – I'd be happy to edit a book about honour killings."

So we had reached a sort of peace, or perhaps rather an armistice. We had a joint assignment, that was how we regarded it. We knew that we wanted to change the way things were, and were willing to do whatever was necessary. It came naturally to us to notice small things which reflected a bigger picture. Such as the fact that women are depicted on Swedish 20- and 50-krona notes, but men are on the 100-, 500- and 1,000-krona ones. Nothing to worry about. Or is it? The Nobel Prize is almost always awarded to a man, Sweden has not yet had a female prime minister, nearly all great inventors and scientists are men, most university professors are men.

Yet at the same time it's men who rape, kill and assault others. One woman in five is subjected to rape or attempted rape during her lifetime. One woman in five! Half the population of the world comprises women, but they own only a tiny bit of the world's resources. Women are hardly represented at all in the corridors of power. No woman has been the U.N. Secretary-General. Everybody knows about Mozart, Vivaldi, Bach. Where are the female composers?

Men write history. Men write about their male friends. For thousands of years there has been a power structure biased in favour of men, and it is hard to change that.

For those who wonder why Stieg refused to change the title of his first novel, *Män som hatar kvinnor* (Men Who Hate Women – it was often changed in translated versions), there you have the answer. Both he and I lived in an environment in which we were constantly reminded of the consequences of this lack of equality, which has always been the norm, and still is. It didn't matter that we were both men – as far as we were concerned, the system was obviously wrong and we felt obliged to correct it.

But now we sat in silence, as if we had just completed twelve rounds in a boxing ring. I felt unsure whether I would be able to get up from the little stool in my corner when the bell rang. But there was something gnawing away inside me. I agreed with everything Stieg said, even if he sometimes tended to go over the top. The fact is that he could sound like other brilliant speakers holding forth about ideals of equality at conferences, in seminars, at demonstrations, in books and in the media.

I ought to have asked him that evening how well he lived up to his feminist visions in the everyday world. When had he last done the laundry? How many of the household chores did he help his partner with? When had he last done the washing up? Whenever I visited him and Eva for dinner he always helped to lay the table, serve the food and contribute to the washing up. I also know that he liked ironing. But it was always obvious that he wasn't the one in charge of the household. It was Eva who took care of everything, from paying the bills to buying the food.

Stieg always claimed that he couldn't cook, although he often promised his friends to serve them roast hare one day. He said that was his signature dish. Unfortunately I was never lucky enough to sample this magnificent meal.

But perhaps it is unfair to make accusations of this kind. Stieg was hardly ever at home, after all. Maybe it is just another regrettable reminder that theory and practice are rarely as close to one another as we would like to think.

There was one thing I couldn't resist bringing up that evening. It was impossible, given the long discussion we had had.

"Stieg, do you remember a question I asked you some three years ago?"

"Which question do you mean?"

"After all you have said this evening, can you explain why there is only one woman on *Expo*'s seven-strong editorial board? It would be easy to conclude that there are not enough competent women in Sweden who could cope with a job on *Expo*."

He didn't even try to defend himself.

"I know. It's my fault. But the fact is I'm always too stressed to do anything about it."

"It's only a matter of time before the media catch on."

He nodded dejectedly.

"I know, I know."

He suddenly looked depressed. That had not been my intention. I was worried, I really was, and I knew the explanation he gave was true. When would he have had time to sort out the gender balance at *Expo*? How many hours are there in a day?

As usual, our arguments had come up against a snag. Yet again we had fought a battle in the office, dealt with important questions that needed sorting out, only to find that shortly thereafter we were back to square one.

The basement windows were just as impenetrably black as before. There was still some time to go before dawn. Nothing outside could be seen clearly from where we were sitting. The world was deaf, vague, unclear and uncertain.

If the night was a rose, it had just scratched us with one of its sharp thorns.

9

The anti-racist as crime novelist

By the time Stieg reached the age of thirty-six, he could begin to call himself an author. Naturally, it never occurred to him to tell anybody else that, but the fact is that for the last fourteen years of his life he was involved in ten different book projects, usually as editor, but sometimes as author. The only non-fiction to appear under his own name is *Överleva deadline – Handbok för hotade journalister* (Surviving the Deadlines – A Handbook for Threatened Journalists), published in 2000 by the Swedish Journalists' Union. The recurring theme in all his technical books is racism, and half of those are about the xenophobic Sweden Democrats.

Stieg's first book was *Extremhögern* (The Extreme Right), a factual study which has become a classic. He wrote it in the spring of 1991 together with the journalist Anna-Lena Lodenius. It was an extremely ambitious survey, 370 pages in length, of organized racism: nothing like it had ever been published in Sweden before. The book comprises twenty chapters, divided into three parts. Geographically it stretches from Sweden to the U.S., and covers the time from the First World War to the present day.

Cooperation between the two authors was not always smooth. Their attitudes towards their subject matter were too different. Stieg refused to compromise and adopt a neutral approach to neo-Nazis, racists and xenophobes. He kept on using words like *madmen, psychopaths, blockheads* and *idiots*. While the writing was in progress, the warrior within him sprang into life once more, and he strode forth looking for trouble. Anna-Lena has told me how difficult it was to work with Stieg. She felt that what these individuals did was more than sufficient to show what kind of people they were, but Stieg wanted to use highly critical or disparaging language to describe intolerant persons and groups. It eventually became impossible for him and Anna-Lena to work together, and after writing the joint foreword to the second edition, their collaboration came to an end.

I have to say that I understand how Stieg could be difficult to work with while writing. Presumably the only way of completing the book was to allow him to use his own vocabulary. Mind you, now – eighteen years later – it strikes me that he and Anna-Lena Lodenius complemented each other perfectly. Stieg had greater insight into the racist movements and an impressively extensive network. There was no doubt about his expertise when it came to racism. The archive he compiled so laboriously was unique. On the other hand, Anna-Lena was in total command of the full range of journalistic skills.

The first part of *Extremhögern* is devoted to the racist and neo-Nazi movements that expanded in Sweden during the 1980s. Part Two, "The International Scene", depicts the growth of racism in Italy, Great Britain, the U.S., France, Germany, Denmark and Norway, and of right-wing extremism in the rest of Europe. The third and final part deals with political violence and criminality linked to the Swedish far right.

The book contains several astonishing analyses of the growth of intolerance, especially in Europe. In a number of countries xenophobic parties have regularly been part of coalition governments.

Unfortunately it is difficult to get hold of a copy today. It never came out in paperback, although the two hardback editions combined sold seven thousand copies. I heard recently that *The Girl Who Kicked the Hornets' Nest* sold two hundred thousand copies in Spain on a single day, 18 July, 2009. There is a certain difference, of course.

Eight years passed before Stieg became involved in a new book project, *Euro-Nat – Ett Europa för antisemiter, etniska krigare och dårfinkar – Sverigedemokraternas internationella nätverk* (Euro-Nat – A Europe for Anti-Semites, Ethnic Warriors and Political Crackpots – The Sweden Democrats' International Network), published in 1999. It is a slim and modest-looking volume with a black and blue cover depicting a map of Europe split down the middle. It looks a bit like a brochure from the local pharmacy. In it, however, Stieg provides a thorough analysis of all the neo-Nazi parties in Belgium, Finland, France, Greece, Italy, Croatia, Portugal, Romania, Serbia, Slovakia, Spain, Sweden, the Czech Republic and Hungary.

His next book, *Överleva deadline*, the Handbook for Threatened Journalists, came as soon as the following year. It comprises four sections of sixty pages each and is devoted to those who have "the world's most dangerous career". He explains ways in which journalists might be threatened, and what help is available. Threats with political overtones, from criminal gangs, angry readers, psychopaths, madmen and opinionated bigots, are analysed in detail. The final part contains an account of journalists under threat all over the world. My copy has a dedication that I shall always treasure: "17 October, 2000. To an obvious source of inspiration in this context, my friend Kurdo".

In his next book project Stieg collaborated with somebody he was very fond of, the journalist Mikael Ekman, who worked on *Expo* and for the television production company Strix. Together they wrote *Sverigedemokraterna – Den nationella rörelsen* (Sweden Democrats – The National Movement), which appeared in 2001. In the preface they establish that the aim of the book is to present "the history of the Sweden Democrats, the party's ideological background and its practical activities".

I often suggested to Stieg that he ought to write books by himself, but he wouldn't listen. It was important for him to keep on finding new collaborators. I could never work out why this was: Stieg was easily annoyed and easily hurt, and was always keen on doing everything his own way.

When he was in the middle of work on a book, he almost became a man possessed. He seemed to have time for nothing else, breathed more heavily, was always in a hurry and smoked non-stop. Moreover, matters on which he and his co-author had agreed could change in the twinkling of an eye. He not infrequently got up on his high horse and rewrote a chapter written by a collaborator. I often saw Stieg change other people's texts, both *Expo* articles and chapters of books. He meant well, but not everybody approved of him asserting himself in this way. I was told a number of times that he hadn't informed the original authors of the changes he had made. That is a pity.

He would do this because he was convinced that the most important thing was for a text to be perfect, even if a few noses were put out of joint along the way. He told me several times that when it came to texts on racism or anti-racism, he was not prepared to give ground on anything.

Once again I have that vision of Stieg as a warrior on a warhorse. Every time a new book project was thrown into the balance, I would tell myself that things would turn out well in the end, the collaborators would become friends again once the book was finished and published. I was usually wrong, although Stieg did seem to become less difficult to work with as the years went by.

No doubt there are several answers to the question why Stieg was always looking for somebody to collaborate with instead of writing his books about intolerance on his own. It would not have been more difficult for him to do so, that is not the reason. Perhaps he wanted to signal to the racists that there were several people keeping an eye on them. Or maybe he wanted to help other writers to move into journalism investigating these disturbing social developments. Of course, it could also be that he was less sure of himself than I and others realized. Perhaps he needed others to push the projects along so that they really were completed. Even a lone wolf might be glad of company now and then.

The most likely explanation is that he was indifferent to seeing his name on the cover of a book. He really was totally lacking in any kind of narcissistic or exhibitionist tendencies. When a book was finished he preferred his co-author to be the one in the spotlight. Stieg avoided television chat shows like the plague.

Another reason for his keenness to find collaborators was that if he did so, he would lose less time and energy on any one project and so could soon turn his attention to something new. He also preferred to work with female journalists, because he thought there were not enough women taking part in the public debate about intolerance. Several times he suggested that he and I should write a book together, but I was never interested. I preferred to be his publisher because I had seen how complicated relations often became between him and his collaborators. I was happy not to become involved in confrontations like that.

But there was another reason. He had ghostwritten so many appeals for which I then received a lot of praise and attention. I didn't have the heart to carry on stealing the limelight from Stieg. I preferred to have him receive the plaudits.

Instead, he turned his attention to another book, *Debatten om hedersmord* (The Honour Killings Debate), of which he was co-editor. It was published in January 2004. Only a few months later he started work on what would be his last work of non-fiction, an anthology on the Sweden Democrats, *Sverigedemokraterna från insidan* (The Sweden Democrats from the Inside), edited by Richard Slätt, who was *Expo*'s assistant editor-in-chief. It was no accident that this book appeared in the summer of 2004. That was the year the Sweden Democrats fielded many candidates in the E.U. elections. The book attracted a great deal of attention in xenophobic magazines and home pages.

The fact is that this was the first book in the *Expo* family for which Stieg didn't take the initiative, though he spent a lot of time and enthusiasm extolling it. I think it was important to him that others were displaying an interest in following in his foot-steps. Perhaps that was also the feeling that encouraged him to dare to devote more of his energy to his fictional writing. He never hid the fact that he thought it was more fun to create his own characters and invent exciting storylines. All the time I knew

Stieg he cherished ambitions to become a writer. The fact that such a lot of people in my circles have always had that dream – which never became reality – meant that I didn't listen 100 per cent to my friend. He first mentioned the fact that he was writing a novel in the autumn of 1997, and I think that was when he wrote the first chapter of *The Girl with the Dragon Tattoo*. But I don't know exactly when he started spending more time on his crime novels. What is clear, however, is that he wrote the best part of them between 2000 and 2003.

Stieg wanted to be a best-selling author. This desire was not just based on the fact that he wanted to earn money – he wanted to earn money in order to realize his dreams of continuing to publish *Expo*, and possibly founding an institution that would keep a constant eye on intolerant organizations. With the aid of sound financial backing, Stieg wanted to change the world. He would use the money he earned from his books to help other people. He had no interest in leading a life of luxury – he had no intention of exchanging his black rucksack for a briefcase!

It also suited his belligerent instincts to tackle big, complicated plots. He always said he found it relaxing to write prose. In the middle of the night he would sit in his office writing while everybody else was in bed. There, in the middle of the night, is where Stieg Larsson the crime novelist was created.

Stieg Larsson wrote specialized non-fiction books for thirteen years, all of which were well informed and played a major role in contemporary political debate among other things. In addition – not many people know this – Stieg had been mad on science fiction since his teens. No doubt the telescope he was presented with as a twelve-year-old contributed to his enthusiasm. It is possible to trace his fondness for the genre by following links to various Swedish libraries. In his twenties, he and Rune Forsgren were the editors of the S.F. magazine *Fijagh*, a stencilled publication produced in five issues between 1974 and 1976. Shortly afterwards he became involved in *Fanac – Science fiction nyhetstidningen* (Fanac – The Science Fiction Newspaper), which he co-edited with Eva from 1978 to 1979. For some time in the 1980s he was chairman of the Scandinavian Association for Science Fiction.

If Stieg Larsson were still alive today he would be an international celebrity. Not for his non-fiction books, but for his crime novels. He would have been pestered day after day with questions like "When did you write the books?", "How much of your own life, your character and your political commitment is in the books?", "Who were the real-life models for Lisbeth Salander and Mikael Blomkvist?"

I can't answer these questions as Stieg would have done. Obviously. But despite my lack of knowledge I might be able to cast a bit of light on some of them. I have no doubt that my friend would have been pleased with my honest attempt to fill in the gaps.

The first question that everybody asked when it became clear that he had written three crime novels, one after the other, intended to be published at one-year intervals, was, "When the hell did he make time to write them?" Everybody who knew Stieg was aware of how hard he worked. Those who weren't were impressed even so, because the effort required to produce a finished book is so immense – how much more effort must have been involved to produce three doorstep-thick novels like the Millennium trilogy in such a short time?

Stieg himself acknowledged that he wrote quickly. "I write as a way of relaxing," he would say every time he spoke about his novel-writing. In the summer of 2003 he started talking more about his work on the crime novels, but he never mentioned the fact that he had already sent the manuscripts to a publishing house. I first heard about that shortly before Christmas 2003, when he let slip in passing that he had sent the text of three novels to the publisher Piratförlag. The main reason he had chosen them was because the company was partly owned by Liza Marklund, who had made her name as a successful crime writer and then shown active support for Stieg in the debate on the oppression of women in 2002. It was a very long time before the publisher got round to responding to Stieg, however, and when they finally did so it was with a curt refusal. Stieg's faith in Liza Marklund was undermined further when he invited her to write a chapter on the oppression of women for *Debatten om hedersmord*. She didn't even reply to his invitation.

Stieg's friend Robert Aschberg, who apart from being an established journalist was also *Expo*'s publisher, had read his books. He recommended them to Norstedts, whose editors, having read the first two novels at one sitting, promptly issued contracts for all three.

While this was happening, Stieg was turning up regularly at the office as usual. We collaborated on several articles. He didn't have much to say about the books.

To be perfectly honest, his reticence made me wonder about their quality. I underestimated him.

Many readers of Stieg's books wonder how much of himself is in the character of Mikael Blomkvist. There are some obvious similarities, of course. They are both journalists and work on magazines critical of contemporary society – even if I imagine that Stieg would have liked to be as good an investigative journalist as his main character.

Apart from that I don't think there are many similarities. I think Stieg had much more in common with Lisbeth Salander, not least their lack of confidence in so-called authorities. And they both had a reluctance to talk about the past. Both of them preferred not to discuss their childhoods. Moreover, they seem to have had similarly bad eating habits. But it has to be said that Mikael Blomkvist didn't appear to be all that interested in cooking either.

In this book I have been quite critical of Stieg as a journalist and reporter. But his weaknesses in that respect were more than made up for by his phenomenal ability to do research. In a way one could say that Lisbeth is Stieg as a researcher, albeit supercharged. She is cleverer and faster than he was – but after all, everything is easier in fiction than in real life.

It is hardly surprising that Stieg made Lisbeth a chain-smoker. It is not difficult to work out where that vice came from. The same applies to her as a drinker of awful coffee.

The Stockholm locations are pretty much accurate – the fact that "Millennium Walks" through the Söder district have been a big hit confirms this.

So it is possible to find reflections of Stieg's everyday life in the novels. In a masterly way he depicted the things about which he was an authority. I think that what makes his books unique is the way in which he portrayed the violent exploitation of women and the forces at work behind that. Readers are aware that these stories are being told by somebody who knew what he was talking about.

Needless to say, there were others who served as models for characters in the books apart from himself. A lot of authors write about how their characters are amalgamations of friends and acquaintances. That is no doubt true in Stieg's case as well. I would go so far as to say that a few of the *Expo* staff are clearly recognizable in the books. And of course, it is only reasonable that a large number of the characters and the inspiration behind the books come from the history and environment of *Expo*. To give a few examples: one of *Expo*'s first members of staff was a well-known, highly competent researcher and computer wizard; a very important person in the history of *Expo* was Jenny, who most probably inspired Lisbeth Salander's appearance, clothes and tattoos; and Mikael Blomkvist's endless philandering is very reminiscent of somebody – who happened also to be called Michael – who worked on *Expo* in the early days.

The fact that I am named and feature in *The Girl Who Kicked the Hornets' Nest* was due to the fact that I was a friend who happened to have been born in Kurdistan. Stieg the internationalist had a warm regard for and interest in the world's forty million stateless Kurds. As soon as he had an opportunity to do so, he called attention to Saddam Hussein's oppression of the Kurds. Many Kurds had great respect for Stieg, thanks to his participation in their long struggle for human rights in Iran, Turkey and Syria.

The important role played by Grenada in *The Girl Who Played with Fire* has to do with Stieg's long-standing and active interest in the little island in the West Indies. It is hardly a coincidence that Lisbeth Salander happens to go there on holiday. In real life Stieg visited the Marxist lawyer and prime minister Maurice Bishop several times. Stieg was also an important member of the Grenada Committee and was associated with its journal in Stockholm. Only a month or so before he died, he and I had dinner at the home of one of his friends from that country. Stieg was delighted to find that nearly all the committee were present.

"Bishop was the Caribbean Che Guevara. He was a friend of mine," Stieg once told me over a glass of whisky. Stieg didn't like it if anybody criticized Bishop, the friend of Cuba and in my view less than perfect – Bishop never allowed a general election and made his mistress Jacqueline Creft a government minister. Both Stieg and I were aware of a bitter fact with regard to Bishop's fate: it was the prime minister's own party that overthrew him and placed him under house arrest a few days before the U.S. invaded Grenada in 1983. Gigantic demonstrations with the slogan "Freedom for Bishop" took place spontaneously in the streets. The revolutionary Bishop, father of three, did not live to see his fortieth birthday. When he was murdered shortly after the invasion, Stieg lent his telephone directory for the capital city, Saint George, to the foreign news desk at T.T., so that they could contact people who could make authoritative statements.

Another question one might ask is why Stieg waited so long before submitting his manuscripts. Why did he complete three whole books before sending them to a publisher? I think the answer is simpler than one might think. Several threads were running parallel inside his head; some of them ended in one book, but others continued through a second one or even all three. He never regarded the novels as separate books but as part of a series. In order to keep control over that enormous amount of material, he probably needed to work on several manuscripts at the same time.

He was also extremely careful about his characters. He came to be very fond of them. Displaying exceptional discipline, he would develop the plot in various sections of several books at the same time, rather than finishing one book before starting the next one. Having finished a chapter of the first book in the series, he would immediately write a chapter in book two, and when that was finished he would do the same in book three. That is what he said he did, and I have no reason to doubt that is what happened. When Stieg was writing his books he was totally absorbed in what he was doing. He was renowned for his memory and for his ability to juggle several balls at the same time. The novels were a way for him to develop this technique to the utmost, keeping all the books inside his head.

How many books would Stieg have written if he had lived longer? I once heard him say quite specifically in a smoke-filled room at the *Expo* offices, "I have ten books in my head."

Somebody else has claimed that Stieg was planning five books. But that is what I heard him say. Stieg had ten books in his head, all of them more or less complete. I am convinced that is precisely what the situation was.

One might also ask where he got all his plots from. Just as several of the characters were based on people in his immediate circle, it is likely that something similar applied to the plots. I suspect that few people have read as many articles and police reports as Stieg had. Tens of years of material were piled up high at home and in his office. The fact is that he read almost all of it very carefully.

During the time he was collecting this material, an average of thirty-six women a year were killed in Sweden by men who knew them well. If you are looking for a focus in Stieg's writing, I would suggest it is the woman's point of view. More or less everything he wrote depicts women being attacked for various reasons; women who are raped, women who are ill-treated and murdered because they challenge the patriarchy. It is this senseless violence that Stieg wanted to do something about and that he refused to accept.

One of the most pressing reasons why Stieg wrote the Millennium trilogy is undoubtedly something that happened in the late summer of 1969. The location was a camping site in Umeå. I have always avoided writing about what took place that day, but it is unavoidable in this context. It affected Stieg so deeply that it became a sombre leitmotif running through all three of his novels.

On that summer's day, fifteen-year-old Stieg watched three friends rape a girl the same age as himself. Her screams were heart-rending, but he didn't intervene. His loyalty to his friends was too strong. He was too young, too insecure. It was inevitable that he would realize afterwards that he could have acted and possibly prevented the rape.

Haunted by feelings of guilt, he contacted the girl a few days later. She lived not far from him and he knew her personally. When he begged her to forgive him for his cowardice and passivity, she told him bitterly that she could not accept his explanations. "I shall never forgive you," she said, through gritted teeth.

That was one of the worst memories Stieg told me about. It was obvious, looking at him, that the girl's voice still echoed in his ears, even after he had written three novels about vulnerable, violated and raped women. Presumably it was not his intention to be forgiven after writing the books, but when you read them it is possible to detect the driving force behind them.

As a result, the women in his novels have minds of their own and go their own ways. They fight! They resist! Just as he wished all women would do in the real world.

Stieg always distanced himself from people who used their positions of power to force weaker people to obey them. That is another underlying and key theme in all his writing: the fight for freedom.

There were two events that shocked Stieg deeply, as well as inspiring his writing. I think it helps with an understanding of Stieg's books, not least *The Girl with the Dragon Tattoo*, if you know the background.

In the mid-1980s Stieg got to know a European anti-racist with an invaluable knowledge of right-wing extremism in Europe. A few years later Stieg heard that this same man had beaten up his partner repeatedly. Stieg the feminist was faced with a difficult choice. Should he break off all contact with the man, despite the fact that he had begged forgiveness for what he had done? The question Stieg was forced to try to answer was whether it was possible to condemn the ill-treatment of women and yet continue to associate with a man who had abused a woman.

Stieg dropped the man. One of Stieg's own weaknesses was that he found it difficult to be reconciled, to forgive and forget with regard to people with whom he had had conflicts.

"Up north, where I come from," he used to say, "you never forgive anybody for anything."

I sometimes understood his refusal to relent, but most often not. If several years have passed since an incident took place, and the person in question has apologized, why can't you forgive and move on? But Stieg could never forgive anybody who failed to give him unconditional friendship, or those who exploited his own unconditional friendship. He wanted to be treated like he treated his friends. As we all know, that seldom happens.

On the other hand, I am convinced that what his friend had done inspired Stieg to put even more energy into his campaign against the oppression of women. In addition, the incident increased his understanding of how complex the whole matter is.

Some years later Stieg was affected by a similar problem, but this time it happened in his own backyard. The best researcher and computer wizard in Sweden had been working at *Expo* for some time. He mesmerized everybody, both on staff and further afield, with his talents, his capacity for work and his social competence. Stieg was most impressed by his enormous talent. Unfortunately their friendship didn't last very long. It soon transpired that the young man had been reported to the police for assault. The news exploded like a bomb in the *Expo* editorial office. Shortly afterwards it became front-page news in the national media.

Worst of all for Stieg was being let down. This was a young man whose relationship with him had been something out of the ordinary. Somebody in the editorial office termed it a father–son relationship. So once again Stieg found himself in a situation where everything he stood for had been challenged by somebody close to him. What should he do? Forgive the younger man?

At the same time as Stieg was fighting this private battle, *Expo* was being pestered non-stop for comments and explanations. And of course the whole business became a long-running story in neo-Nazi, racist and xenophobic publications. In the end Stieg and *Expo* decided they had no choice but to sever all contact with the young researcher.

It is no exaggeration to say that this incident developed into a trauma for Stieg. He could never understand how he could have misjudged one of his closest colleagues so fundamentally. Never before had his strict principle been challenged in such a flagrant way – the motto that dictated everything else in his life: *Respect everybody, regardless of their skin colour, gender, language, religion, ethnic background or sexual orientation. Always. In all circumstances. Unconditionally.*

I am quite certain that this researcher is linked with Lisbeth Salander's abilities. How do I know? The answer is obvious if one goes back several years. The researcher was forced to leave *Expo* in 1997. As I already mentioned, that was the year when Stieg wrote his first chapter about Lisbeth Salander. Stieg dealt with his sorrow and disappointment by creating a character similar to the researcher. I think my friend wanted to salve his own wounds by doing something that is not all that unusual: allowing a person to cause damage in the imagination rather than in the real world. One summer's day in 2009 I bumped into the researcher from *Expo*. I shall never forget the first thing he said: "Stieg got his revenge in his own way. I am Lisbeth Salander as far as her computer expertise is concerned. And we are both slender and don't weigh enough! But I shall always love Stieg. It's an honour to be a model for Salander."

Quite early on in his time at T.T. Stieg was made the new agency's crime-fiction specialist. This wasn't especially surprising. He had read practically everything that had been written in that genre for the past two hundred years. But he didn't write much about it for T.T. Their archive contains three of his articles on the subject of crime novels for summer reading, two on crime novels to read at Christmas and two other similar pieces. Most of these recommend recently published books.

The list of titles makes it easy to see where Stieg got his inspiration. Names that keep cropping up include Erskine Childers, Norman Mailer, Arthur Conan Doyle, Agatha Christie, James Ellroy, John Buchan, John le Carré, Tom Clancy, Frederick Forsyth, Peter Høeg and Mark Frost. What is most obvious is that he preferred several female crime writers. His favourites were Minette Walters, Patricia Cornwell, Liza Cody, Sue Grafton, Val McDermid, Dorothy Sayers and Sara Paretsky.

He also interviewed two authors. The first was the science-fiction writer Harlan Ellison, whose output included scripts for Alfred Hitchcock films, *Batman*, *The Man from U.N.C.L.E.* and *Star Trek*. Ellison and Stieg certainly had things in common. They both lived under constant threat of being murdered and they both became successful crime writers.

But it is the other interview which is most interesting. In September 1992, Stieg either met or conducted a telephone interview with the crime writer Elizabeth George. It is clear that she was a major source of inspiration for him; among other things he called her the queen of crime writing. It is not difficult to imagine that Stieg's relationship with the genre would have been very different without books like *A Great Deliverance, Payment in Blood, A Suitable Vengeance* and *Well-Schooled in Murder*.

Stieg told me how pleased he was once his work with Norstedts got under way. One reader's report was written by Lasse Bergström, now retired but formerly in charge of publishing. Bergström described the first volume as an orthodox crime novel with a self-contained mystery, the second as a police thriller and the third as a political thriller.

Stieg replied to Bergström's comments in an email to his publisher, Eva Gedin:

> Please tell Lasse Bergström that he's obviously an intelligent and sensible person of impeccable taste, and that flattery will get him everywhere. Hmm. I don't know, but I have the impression that you Norstedts people are seriously enthusiastic about my books. O.K., I know they are not bad, and of course I'm delighted to read such flattering judgements; but I hope that, for whatever reason, you are not holding back negative comments. I'm quite capable of coping with criticism. It's most satisfying to see that Lasse noticed that I changed the genre from one novel to the next. He caught on to exactly what I was trying to do.

Being the inveterate reader of crime novels that he was, Stieg had decided to develop his characters over a series of books. But that wasn't all. He also played with the genre by letting the stories unfold in different styles. Flair of that order of course demands a precise knowledge of what you are doing. It wouldn't surprise me if this clever device is one of the reasons why readers the world over have been fascinated by the Millennium trilogy.

There is a rumour suggesting that Stieg wrote crime stories as early as the 1990s, but destroyed them. Is it true? Yes and no. The fact is that he did indeed write crime stories in the mid-90s – but they were not what later became *The Girl with the Dragon Tattoo, The Girl Who Played with Fire* and *The Girl Who Kicked the Hornets' Nest*. It was more a case of him writing in order to relax and have fun. The natural outcome was that he developed as a writer during that period. Alongside writing, the biggest pleasure in his life was doubtless reading. He devoured books, both nonfiction and crime novels. He was something of a literary omnivore. He read pulp literature as well as Dostoevsky, Zola and heavy Greek philosophers. Stieg liked mysteries, which is why he found it hard to lead a life lacking in crime fiction.

You could call those early stories practice crime novels. He told me they were utterly worthless. I find that hard to believe, even if they were far less accomplished than the books he eventually published. But we will never know the truth.

On the other hand, the determination with which he destroyed all his earlier attempts shows that he was aware that he had now accomplished something worthwhile. I don't think success would have come as a complete surprise to him. In any case, he saw enough of the attention his first crime novel attracted before it was published to suspect that something major was about to happen. Not many authors have three books accepted, discover that a "buzz" has developed around them well before the first one is published, and even take part in negotiations for film contracts and foreign rights.

So far the Millennium trilogy has earned over a million kronor. Stieg Larsson has become a class-A celebrity. People beg me to sign his books in Madrid, Barcelona and Paris – simply because I was one of his friends! The films based on his books are breaking records all over Europe. Reporters travel from as far away as Argentina to Stockholm in order to write about Stieg.

The question is how he would have reacted to the enormous attention he and his books have attracted.

I have thousands of examples of how Stieg shied away from publicity, especially the kind that placed him in the spotlight. He always preferred to let somebody else do that, but he was a realistic person in all circumstances. I am convinced he would have agreed to take part in television programmes and given interviews – but only the ones he really wanted to do. Most requests would certainly have been turned down. I'm sure he would have preferred to feature in small underground magazines rather than on the main television channels and in daily newspapers. That's simply the kind of person he was.

I don't think he would have changed much in his way of life as a result of the enormous income his books have produced. He would have continued to smoke his cigarettes, eat badly, sleep hardly at all and write more books. Above all else he would have continued to keep a very sharp eye on intolerant groups and individuals. What else he would have spent his fortune on I can't say – that would be pure speculation, and I would rather avoid engaging in it.

Stieg's success has also changed my life. I am often invited to lecture about him throughout Europe. I am interviewed more or less every day by journalists from all over the world, and am invited to attend Stieg's film premières on every corner of the Continent. Sometimes I attend these events, but at other times I turn them down. It feels almost as if, in a most bizarre fashion, I have become an ambassador for Stieg. But I do it willingly and must admit that I feel very happy to have him in my orbit in this way. It's not how I would have wanted things to turn out. I would have preferred to continue sitting in a basement office with my friend, and to carry on producing a journal with a less than adequate budget. But I can't turn the clock back. Stieg has left my life as a living person. Every time I meet somebody who has become a little happier after having read one of his novels, though, I also become a little happier. In that way he is always present. And it is a presence full of memories that nobody can take away from me.

10

Successes and setbacks

A memory. Stieg in the bar at Södra Teatern one very pleasant June evening in 2003. He orders a double whisky, a group of revellers breaks into song, people are crowded together in the cramped space, the place is buzzing with carefree voices, meaningful looks are exchanged. The terrace door is open, letting a modicum of cool air into the smoke-filled bar. Stieg lights a cigarette and inhales deeply, then takes a swig of whisky. His constant companion, the black rucksack, is slung over his left shoulder.

I am surprised to note that he seems to have abandoned his classical "neutral" hairstyle. His hair has been cut shorter than usual. And he has acquired sideburns. The new haircut suits him. Makes him look younger. Which is more than one can say for his baggy white T-shirt. Presumably it is a present given to him as a souvenir of a lecture he delivered to some idealistic organization or other somewhere in Sweden. And his jumper has a big red stain.

Stieg is in an exceptionally good mood and waves a greeting to several people who pass by. Standing on his right is a bearded man by the name of Anders, known to everybody as Anders the Trotskyist. He has a baby in his arms. I know Anders. He is one of the organizers of this multicultural evening.

I'm standing in the doorway to the terrace when I catch sight of Stieg. Just as he takes out his pack of cigarettes and a lighter I tap him on the shoulder. He seems pleased to see me.

"This is a fun evening," he says. "Did you know that Anders

and I have known each other ever since the Vietnam demonstrations?"

I shake my head, but am not especially surprised. He orders a glass of red wine and stands there looking at the lovely little baby.

"Here we have a future warrior," he says.

"You always look so young, Stieg," says Anders.

The woman crime novelist is also here this evening. Stieg turns round and catches sight of her. Her first book was published a month or two previously. Even I know how much Stieg helped her to produce her final text.

Her face lights up the moment she sees him.

Mourning involves being haunted by images that take possession of you when you least expect it. It is often impossible to understand why you remember things in such detail, almost as if you were in the same place at the time they happened. You see everything so clearly, inhale the smells and hear the voices.

How you manage to fit together these fragments of memory is probably the basis for mourning. It's a healing process. Why do I recall that evening at the theatre in Söder in such minute detail? I don't know.

Perhaps because I bumped into that woman crime novelist only the other day. I didn't like the fact that her body language often showed that she thought she was a better writer than Stieg. But I no longer hold that against her. After his death she wrote in her blog about how much he had meant to her. She even explained how he had gone through her manuscripts chapter by chapter, sentence by sentence, and helped her.

It was round about the time of that multicultural evening at

Södra Teatern that I made a crucial decision. I had grown thoroughly sick and tired of everything associated with producing magazines. I had devoted all my energy to doing just that for seventeen long years. Now I had run out of energy, and I made up my mind to close down my beloved *Svartvitt*.

I had plans to continue my cooperation with *Expo*, but to be honest I was not at all sure how that would work out. My health had deteriorated steadily during the previous year, and it sometimes felt as if I had spent more time in hospital than in my office.

My doctors said I was displaying all the symptoms of burnout. Nobody can explain exactly what that term means. In my case it was a bit more straightforward than usual: I had absolutely no private life whatsoever.

When I told Stieg about my decision, he was sorry to hear it at first. He tried to talk me out of it, but gave up when he realized that I simply didn't have the strength any more. In a way I suppose we both felt that the areas we had been covering in *Svartvitt* had started to feature in the mainstream media. But we were in complete agreement about continuing our cooperation within *Expo*. I said that my hope was to work on *Expo* as publisher and as a polemical journalist.

"We are not twenty-year-olds any more," I said. "Both you and I must start thinking about our health."

He nodded, but that was a subject in which he had no interest at all. Unlike me he was alert and always busy with several projects at the same time. The fact is that apart from my closing down *Black and White*, 2003 was a comparatively quiet year. There were no real threats, no headline-grabbing manoeuvres aimed at us, no complicated books to publish, nothing of that kind.

Naturally, we ought to have realized that it was the calm before the storm.

The following year, 2004, things happened in rapid succession. It started positively for Stieg. He was on the way to enjoying the fruits of all those sleepless nights and hard work. In the space of four months he put the finishing touches to five books, more books than he had produced during the previous forty-nine years of his life. An astonishing achievement.

As early as 22 January *Debatten om hedersmord* appeared. In April Stieg signed the contract with Norstedts for the publication of the three books that would become the Millennium trilogy. The very next month he worked on two central chapters of *Sverigedemokraterna från insidan*. He gave a lot of talks to schools and also travelled to Brussels for a conference. A paper in connection with an exhibition in Malmö took up much of his energy in the autumn. The fact is that our last conversation was about that paper, which I reckoned he should have delegated to somebody else.

In addition, it seemed that his successes were making him more extrovert than he had ever been before. He took on more and more, and went out to meet people more regularly. He became a familiar face at Café Fix, Café Anna, Café Copacabana, Café Mellqvist and Il Caffè. Although he had always felt more at home in small groups, he started to move in bigger circles and became one of the in-crowd. He was a frequent guest at the so-called multicultural events on the terrace at Södra Teatern, and stayed on until surprisingly late.

Needless to say, a lot of people continued to ask for his help and advice. A teacher in Sollentuna wanted to launch a new curriculum subject, "Tolerance and Respect". Students asked him to read and comment on their essays about neo-Nazism or racism. Social workers responding to attacks on women needed help in various ways. And another would-be crime novelist required assistance with a manuscript.

I frequently asked myself what was going on. What had happened to Stieg's non-stop work into the early hours? The new Stieg was barely recognizable. He had always used to slip away at the earliest opportunity in order to glue himself to his computer in peace and quiet.

I suppose it was because he had received the message he wanted to hear most of all just then. He had received confirmation that all those exhausting hours spent at the computer with his enormously long novels had been worthwhile. He had not misjudged the quality of his work. It really was good. Perhaps around this time he even began to think that his books were more than just good. Perhaps they were very special indeed.

This was probably the first time in his adult life when he could relax and felt that he could allow himself some late nights of pleasure. He could take time off.

I hope that was in fact the case. I really do think it was.

Sometimes I find myself smiling at the probability that the baggy T-shirts I so disliked were a part of this process. By shedding his jacket and tie perhaps he was building up his image as a writer. A sort of circle had closed. The slipshod working-class lad had progressed to reserved austerity and had now returned to being slipshod.

What finally convinced me that he had changed was when he suddenly started agreeing to be interviewed, and to think giving lectures was boring. To my great delight, he agreed to take part on 24 July in a live chat show on Swedish television. The last time he had appeared on live T.V. had been 24 April, 1991.

When I look back at 2004, I realize that an awful lot happened. On 27 June, Stieg rang sounding breathless. He was very insistent that I should place an article in one of the dailies about the secretary of a political party with neo-Nazi leanings. The man in question had assaulted his partner on several occasions.

I recall him saying "on several occasions" over and over again, stressing the phrase every time. Shortly afterwards he emailed me the text as an attachment. I cut about half of it, then sent it out. The following day it was published in *Expressen*.

I had only just seen it when Stieg rang me on his mobile.

"Well done. The radio people have just been on the phone," he said, also mentioning that, as usual, he didn't expect to be paid for the article.

Nevertheless, I recall feeling rather worried after that phone call. I thought he had started sounding stressed again, under pressure. I wondered if it might be linked to a review of *Debatten om hedersmord*. A leader writer on *Dagens Nyheter* had written a piece about it that was dismissive, to say the least. The whole article was malicious in tone, and the reviewer attacked Stieg, questioning his motives. She referred to "oddities in an odd book". She was very negative about the choice of the nine experts, who, in her view, churned out the same message about the causes and forms of the oppression of women.

As the publisher, I also received my share of her criticism, which while pungent and malicious was not totally unjustified.

She reserved her strongest vitriol for Stieg's co-editor, Cecilia Englund. Cecilia was accused point blank of publishing something that was untrue. She claimed to have been in touch with a specialist on Islam whom she quoted in the book, but when the leader writer checked, that appeared not to have been the case. This created a major crisis of confidence for Stieg, Cecilia and me. Not to mention the publishing house. Stieg went through the roof and wanted me, as the publisher, to write a response to the leader writer. I declined to do so. As a result he immediately wrote a piece that was signed by all nine contributors to the book. It was refused by *Dagens Nyheter*, which made him even more furious, if that was possible.

In a way it also resulted in Stieg becoming confused. He claimed that there was a dictatorship preventing the free expression of opinions. In fact, the subsequent debate led to him and his supporters being accused of trying to impose just such a dictatorship by citing all kinds of theories as to why the oppression of immigrant women was being suppressed.

The whole debate was a mess. It was also a result of other incidents that had taken place earlier in the year. On 11 March we had all donned our best suits in order to attend the inauguration of the Centre Against Racism. It was in fact Stieg's appeal to the prime minister five years previously that had led to the foundation of this new institution in Sveavägen, in central Stockholm.

Nevertheless, neither Stieg nor I was welcomed with open arms. We shrugged that off, maintaining that the important thing was that the centre had come into being. But deep down we were both rather offended.

In September the bomb I had been warning about for so long

finally exploded. Stieg phoned and said curtly, "Have you seen the article about us employing only men at *Expo*?"

"No," I said with a sigh.

"We're in the shit."

Of course we were. There was an article in a weekly magazine under the less than flattering headline "Only white men at *Expo*". And the content was exactly what we had feared: how *Expo* didn't employ women or Swedes with an immigrant background.

Stieg had given an interview and made a bold attempt to save the situation. But he wasn't very successful. *Expo* had an obvious credibility problem, and he ought to have simply apologized, regretting the situation, and promised to put matters right.

Instead he suggested that it seemed unfortunate that so few immigrants had any interest in questioning nationalist movements. And he added for good measure, "But we have had our nigger-in-chief, Kurdo Baksi, as publisher."

I thought he must have been under a lot of stress when the interviewer phoned him. It didn't sound like Stieg at all. Then it occurred to me that what he needed was some peace and quiet. I wanted to tell him that his body was not made of iron. He needed to rest.

He called and apologized for what he had said about me. Then he seemed to find a new source of energy.

"We'll be getting lots of women and immigrants on *Expo*, just you wait and see."

Oddly enough, it was only a couple of days later that we met and he showed me the first interview he had given as a crime novelist. *Svensk Bokhandel*, the Swedish book trade journal, had carried a long article about the books he was about to publish.

The very headline stopped me in my tracks: "A man for the history books". It was impossible not to see how thrilled Stieg was. All I felt when I read the text was incredible pride and happiness. There was one sentence which attracted my particular attention. It was a quotation from Stieg: "I can tell you that this is my pension insurance."

I have often wondered why I keep thinking back to that evening at Södra Teatern. Perhaps it was the look on Stieg's face. It's so easy to read things into a situation with hindsight. Or maybe it is to do with my thinking that I'd noticed a slackening off in his strict working practices. That I thought this was somehow liberating. His new way of dressing, perhaps – even if I didn't think much of it, it did nevertheless suggest a sort of step forward.

But now, afterwards. Now that we know. The comment that his crime novels were a sort of pension insurance. I've no doubt he didn't say that to trivialize his writing. He would never have done that. But I can't help thinking that he knew what was going to happen, even then. The success lying in store for him.

He never experienced it, as we all know.

In my life the year 2004 stands out as a sort of watershed. I can divide up so many things into what happened before then and what happened afterwards. That year 2004, which as far as Stieg was concerned consisted of just 312 days.

11

Farewell

November was always the most important month in my relation-ship with Stieg. It was the time when the matters he and I were most concerned with were at the forefront of most people's minds in Sweden, so we met more often than usual. If you go through the appeals and articles we wrote, you will find that most of them were written in November.

The first time we ever met with nobody else present was in November. We made a public announcement about the planned cooperation between *Svartvitt* and *Expo* in November. And of course, there is also the date that will always be connected with our work: 30 November, the anniversary of the death of the Swedish warrior-king Charles XII in 1718, a day hijacked by the nationalists for their annual celebrations.

November is not a month you can rely on. Some years ago a group of neo-Nazis shot at my flat in November. It is as if every-thing horrible in my life happens during that month, when the Swedish winter makes the days dark and gloomy. It's said that Swedes always talk about the weather, and I have to agree that it's true. But they are dependent on the weather, and the climate is cruel. In October it is just about possible for brief spells of life-giving Indian summer to interrupt the nasty, damp autumn weather and brighten up people's minds. But November is ruthless, relentless and without compromise. Everybody knows that five months of darkness lie in store.

That in itself should be sufficient to explain why November is a month that makes you grit your teeth. I am one of many who sort of retire into themselves and become that little bit more grumpy and miserable.

I was planning a seminar that Stieg and I would be leading on 9 November. It was the anniversary of Kristallnacht, the Jewish pogrom carried out by German Nazis during the night of 9–10 November, 1938. It is important to remember that event, because in many ways it was the occasion when the world passed the point of no return. Jewish shops and synagogues were destroyed, about twenty thousand Jews were rounded up, and many of them were never heard of again. The world was confronted by a moment of destiny and did nothing about it.

That is why Stieg and I were keen to arrange a seminar every year on that date. As I was sitting in my office, putting the finishing touches to arrangements for the evening, Stieg turned up. I have spoken to the people who were present and they have told me in detail what happened. His old friend Jim from Grenada was waiting for him outside. There was some administrative matter Jim needed help with and Stieg had promised to see what he could do.

"You don't look too good," was the first thing Jim had said.

Stieg shrugged and said, "Come on, let's take the lift."

They discovered that the lift wasn't working. They began trudging laboriously up the seven flights of stairs. Stieg wasn't exactly in peak condition, but now he was breathing even more heavily than usual. When they finally reached the *Expo* editorial offices, he could hardly breathe.

As soon as his old colleague Per saw how pale Stieg was, he decided to call an ambulance. But before anybody could get to the telephone Stieg had collapsed on to the shoulder of a new member of the *Expo* staff, Monika. A few seconds later he slumped to the floor. His heart was still beating.

The ambulance arrived quickly and Stieg was lifted on to a stretcher. The first thing they did was to fix an oxygen mask over his face. The crew worked quickly and efficiently – it was obvious they assumed Stieg had suffered a heart attack. Per travelled with him in the ambulance, which headed for St Göran's Hospital. The ambulance men asked Per how old Stieg was. At which point Stieg lifted up the mask and bawled out, "I'm fifty, damn it!"

I was still in my office when Richard Slätt, *Expo*'s assistant editor-in-chief, phoned.

"Stieg is ill," he said. "He's on his way to St Göran's Hospital. No doubt he won't be able to come to the seminar this evening."

I didn't realize the implications of that telephone call. Like everybody else who receives that kind of message, I tried to assess Richard's tone of voice. He seemed quite calm and collected, which reassured me. I was well aware of course that Stieg would never choose to go to hospital of his own volition, but on the other hand, both of us had needed to go for check-ups in the recent past. No big deal. I did wonder about a heart attack; I have to say that only a couple of days previously I had read an article with the ominous headline "Men between fifty and sixty run the biggest risk of dying from a heart attack".

But it had never occurred to me that this might apply to Stieg. Yes, he worked under pressure all the time; yes, he had all the characteristic symptoms. But even so, he still looked like an overgrown schoolboy.

Besides, it wasn't so long ago that, feeling a bit down after yet another hospital visit, I had jokingly suggested that he should give a lively speech at my funeral. We'd both had a good laugh at that, as one does.

After the call from Richard I continued to put the finishing touches to the preparations for that evening's event at the Swedish W.E.A. Stieg's enforced absence meant that there was more for me to do, but I thought I'd be able to get round that. I decided not to telephone the police and ask for special protection: it should be sufficient to warn the organizers that quite a few neo-Nazis would turn up. I didn't tell them that Stieg was unable to attend, but asked them to make sure that some extra security staff were on duty in the lecture room.

Having replaced the receiver after talking to the organizers, I thought about Stieg again. It struck me that it was only eleven days since I had replaced him as the main speaker at an event in Söderhamn. But when we had met only a couple of days ago, he had been in excellent spirits. He had given me a copy of the interview *Svensk Bokhandel* had published with Stieg Larsson the crime novelist. I had been surprised.

"Will the book be out as early as next June?" I had asked.

Surely he can't fall ill now, I thought. He has too many irons in the fire. Things he has longed to experience all his life. I stood up and walked over to the window. But there again, a hospital visit can act as a wake-up call. He must calm down, enjoy the fact that his novel is shortly going to appear in the bookshops.

I returned to planning the seminar. It would turn out all right. I was used to playing multiple roles and, after all, we had done it several times before.

No, I didn't take Stieg's illness seriously. I knew that in the mid-1970s he had collapsed in Addis Ababa and been in a coma for several hours. He eventually discovered that he had a kidney infection. No doubt it would be something similar this time.

At 6.00 p.m. I officially opened the seminar despite the absence of the star turn. There were about a hundred people in the lecture room; eighty of them were known neo-Nazis.

The mood soon became strained, and several Holocaust survivors were uncertain whether or not they dared to stay on. I had to fight hard to ensure that it would be possible to complete the seminar – but I had no intention of cancelling or suspending it. I had never done so before and was not going to do so this time. I gave my introductory talk on Kristallnacht, and that was followed by two talks on the current mood of xenophobia in Sweden. Then came a question-and-answer session that was anything but easy to control. I was completely exhausted when I rather brusquely wound up proceedings at the advertised time, 7.10 p.m.

The volunteer security men helped me to leave the premises quickly. A few people I had promised to meet for a glass of wine after the seminar were waiting in the Indian restaurant on the ground floor. They asked where Stieg was, and I told them that unfortunately he had been held up at the last minute. Shortly afterwards, I checked my mobile. It was now 7.16 – I remember that clearly. It is as if etched into my memory. That was when I heard the brief recorded message.

"Stieg is dead."

I raced outside and was lucky enough to get a taxi to St Göran's Hospital immediately. The journey took only a few minutes. All the time the words were echoing round my head. Stieg is dead. It can't be true, I thought. I must have misheard it. There must be some kind of mistake.

When I entered the hospital waiting room, I found the *Expo* staff sitting there, all staring into space. They told me that Stieg's family had been informed. Per had phoned from the ambulance and told Eva and Erland that Stieg was seriously ill and on his way to hospital. Stieg's father had immediately raced to Umeå airport in order to catch the first available flight to Stockholm. And Eva was on her way from Falun.

The silence was tangible.

More friends turned up, and there were soon about twenty of us sitting there, comforting one another. But most of the time we sat in silence. Several people didn't seem to have grasped what had happened. The hospital staff served us coffee and ginger biscuits. In my confused state I was unable to make out their faces. They were simply grey shadows wafting past. But suddenly I heard a woman say in a calm tone of voice, "You can say farewell to your friend now."

I was unable to lift my gaze and see exactly where the voice came from. The ground was shifting under my feet. Everything was so improbable. What was I doing there? What had really happened? I wanted to stand up and tell her she couldn't do this. She couldn't simply appear and say something like that. *You can say farewell to your friend now*. It seemed so cruel, so final.

For me there is a life before and a life after that sentence.

It was that sentence which robbed me of my friend in a concrete, brutal and naked way.

It is so absurd. My first thought was how we were soon going to celebrate, after the event, Stieg's fiftieth birthday. Fragments of memories staggered through my mind. I saw him before me on New Year's Eve, 2000, at the home of a colleague somewhere in southern Stockholm, not far from *Expo*'s first office. Then the two of us on the balcony of his home. We were smoking cigarettes, drinking whisky and talking. What were we talking about? What on earth were we talking about? Then our first joint press conference, when he dealt with all the journalists and photographers with his inimitable charm.

I realized that I was crying. I had lost my mentor, and my best discussion partner – but most of all I had lost my unconditional friend. My big brother.

Eva arrived. Naturally, she was heartbroken. We embraced. Shortly afterwards Erland arrived from Umeå. By then it was 9.00 p.m. Still nobody had gone in to say farewell to Stieg.

I was the first to enter the final room Stieg occupied on this earth. He was lying on the bed. He was nicely dressed. He was wearing his glasses. His black and white tie was in place. His eyes were shut. I couldn't grasp that this man had left us.

There was a little stool at the side of the bed. Should I sit there? I walked hesitantly towards Stieg. I clasped my hands together and listened to my own voice.

"Stieg, you are leaving your nearest and dearest very early in life. I want to thank you for all the good times we had together. And for all the difficult ones. I hope I have never hurt you, ever."

Over and over again I had to wipe away tears with the back of my hand.

I was not as strong as I had thought. I left Stieg with slow, stumbling steps.

The others went in to say their farewells. Some went in alone, others in small groups. The last person to say farewell to Stieg was Eva.

Deep down inside me I could hear Stieg's voice repeating the last words he ever said: "I'm fifty, damn it!"

His last words which I didn't actually hear myself. Nevertheless, I could hear them echoing inside me. This was the end of his fifty-year-long journey. A journey that began in Skelleftehamn and continued through his childhood in Bjursele and Sandbacka, and his youth in Umeå, with a few excursions to Eritrea, Morocco, Algeria, Gibraltar, Grenada.

A journey that came to an end one chilly November night at St Göran's Hospital in Stockholm.

No. November is not a month to be relied upon. But, I thought, the considerate Stieg Larsson no doubt had a good reason for leaving when he did. As he almost always had. As usual, I realized that I trusted him, no matter what happened. It could quite simply be, I thought to myself, that his mother, Vivianne, his grandfather Severin and his grandmother Tekla had been kept waiting for him far too long.

Yes, I know, Stieg, it may be a naive thought, but as I write these words I think that despite everything, one of these days we can win peace. We can. All of us. I hope so.

Sleep well, Stieg.

Afterword

This is not a blind tribute to a friend. Everybody who met Stieg Larsson will have their own picture of him. The same applies to those who were close to him.

For more than ten years Stieg and I met almost every day. I was with him during his most difficult times, and I was present and able to share in his successes and happiness.

Despite the fact that he was eleven years older than I, we were colleagues and friends. You could almost say that we were each other's boss. Stieg was the most unassuming person I have ever met, and the unconditional friendship he gave me is irreplaceable.

As his enormous success as a novelist grows, there is a danger that his single-minded fight does not receive the attention it deserves. That fight was such an important part of him, both as a person and as a writer. My hope is that to some extent this book has succeeded in describing it.

It is only now, after almost five years of mourning, that I have been able to summon up enough courage to write about my friend and colleague. This book is my picture of Stieg Larsson.

In conclusion I would like to thank Håkan Bravinger and Eva Gedin at Norstedts for all their help and advice.

Kurdo Baksi
September 2009